READING

FOR SUCCESS

A SCHOOL-TO-WORK APPROACH

Raymond F. Morgan

Professor of Reading Education
Old Dominion University
Norfolk, VA

Mark A. Forget

Instructional Specialist
Virginia Beach Public Schools
Virginia Beach, VA

Joseph C. Antinarella

English Instructor
Tidewater Community College
Chesapeake, VA

SOUTH-WESTERN EDUCATIONAL PUBLISHING

Editor-in-Chief:	Peter McBride
Project Manager:	Laurie Wendell
Editor:	Edna D. Stroble
Production Coordinator:	Tricia Boies
Marketing Manager:	Carolyn Love
Internal Design:	Ann Small
Photo Editor:	Sam Marshall
Cover Design:	Joseph Pagliaro

Copyright © 1996
by SOUTH-WESTERN EDUCATIONAL PUBLISHING
Cincinnati, Ohio

I(T)P
International Thomson Publishing

South-Western Educational Publishing is a division of International Thomson
Publishing, Inc. The ITP trademark is used under license.

ISBN: 0-538-63717-X

3 4 5 6 7 8 9 0 VH 00 99 98

Printed in the United States of America

Library of Congress Cataloging-in-Publication Data

Morgan, Raymond F.
    Reading for success : a school-to-work approach / Raymond F.
Morgan, Mark A. Forget, Joseph C. Antinarella.
      p.   cm.
    Includes bibliographical references (p.) and index.
    ISBN 0-538-63717-X
    1. Reading comprehension. 2. Study skills. 3. Content area
reading. 4. English language—Rhetoric. I. Forget, Mark A., 1948-
. II. Antinarella, Joseph C. 1953-   . III. Title.
LB1050.45.M67 1996   95-24414
372.4'1—dc20   CIP

Preface

Reading for Success introduces students to reading and writing skills that are relevant, practical, and engaging. This unique text focuses on reading a wide variety of print forms immediately applicable to student experience. Students receive instruction and practice in reading textbooks, technical and work-related materials, graphical information, and narratives.

Who Should Read This Book

This textbook provides opportunities for students and adults to learn strategies for more effective reading, writing, and thinking. This textbook is appropriate for readers of all abilities. The authors' experiences teaching these strategies in content area classrooms have attested to this. Students whose abilities are already advanced have testified that their skills have become refined and extended and that the critical thinking skills in many cases were new to them. Students of lesser ability frequently discover for the first time true success in areas they either thought were too difficult or for which they had little interest.

Special Features Of This Textbook

This textbook is meant to be used in conjunction with instruction in any content area classroom. A unique feature of this textbook is the practice it provides with real passages in textbook, technical, and narrative-type readings. This book is different from traditional reading improvement textbooks because it does not emphasize a "workbook" approach. Rather it is based on the belief that real learning takes place in the context of real subject matter of real life. This text challenges the reader to develop skills we believe are inherent in human nature and yet frequently remain dormant. Examples include curiosity, desire to communicate, ability to perform higher level thinking, and the general desire for success. Readers are encouraged to apply the strategies they learn in this book to many technical or academic materials with which they currently work.

Other key features of the text include:

- Reading-plus. Although the text's emphasis in on reading, Writer's Workshops at the end of each chapter provide students with the opportunity to develop their writing skills.

- Active learning. Approaches and activities encourage excitement, fun, group learning, and problem solving. Students are engaged in what they learn.

- Flexible lessons. The text follows a logical, developmental sequence of topics, but is designed so that teachers can pick and choose from the table of contents. Allows maximum flexibility for students and teachers.

- Related skills. Conventional reading skills are included: previewing and prereading, contextual clues, note taking, problem solving, thinking skills, speed reading, and vocabulary development. Students are exposed to a wide array of techniques.

Organization Of This Book

The organization of each of the nine chapters allows the reader to use a complete learning process. First the reader is prepared through objectives and an opening activity. Special activities in reading and writing are strategically placed throughout the chapter to assist the reader in clarifying understanding. Finally, summaries and end-of-chapter activities enhance comprehension and allow the reader to reflect on and apply what has been learned.

Instructor's Manual

The Instructor's Manual that accompanies this text lays a thorough framework for this reading and writing approach. The manual includes a metacognitive abilities test, lesson plans, teaching suggestions, assessment tools, and additional student activities.

Acknowledgments

We extend thanks to our colleagues who encouraged us in this endeavor. Special thanks to the folks at the School-Within-A-School at Green Run High School in Virginia Beach: Brian Alexander, Cindy Edwards, Jeanne Harmon. They helped us to fully test these strategies. Also thanks should go to our teaching colleagues at Bellport Middle School who provided a wealth of ideas and activities, our friends at Bayside High School who encouraged us to see a need for a book like this, and the faculty at Tidewater Community College who support the teaching of reading for success. Thanks should go also to Jean Ingold and the Cox High School ninth grade reading class for their review of the manuscript. Additional thanks go to the following persons with the Virginia Beach Schools who provided support: Jerry Deviney, Lorna Roberson, Don Stowers.

Thanks also to the following reviewers for their feedback and guidance:

- Dr. Mary Kisner, The Pennsylvania State University
- Mary Cagle, Richardson High School, Richardson, TX
- Dr. Russ White and the instructors of Wilmington School District, Wilmington, IL

Our writing was a more pleasant experience because of the support and kind assistance of our manuscript preparer Donna Betts.

Ray Morgan
Mark Forget
Joe Antinarella

Dedications

Ray Morgan:

To my friend and mentor, Franklin Ross Jones, for always encouraging me to excel.

Mark Forget:

To my wife, Karen, and my four boys, Jon, Ian, Nathan, and Andrew for their untiring support of and tolerance for my work.

Joe Antinarella:

To my loving wife, Jo Anne, who is a source of strength; Justin, who sees the humor in life; Cara, who always finds her way; and Casey, who gives of herself.

Table of Contents

Preparing to Read for Success

CHAPTER

1

As you read this chapter, focus your attention on the following objectives. You may wish to refer back to these during your reading. After completing Chapter One, you will be able to:

● understand how to use this book.

● better predict what will be in a textbook chapter.

● use the three steps of reading.

● use a checklist to assess your strengths in reading and locate areas where you can learn to improve.

● make summaries of what you read.

Chapter Outline

I. Getting Ready to Read This Book

II. Why Read a Book to Learn How to Read a Book?

III. The Three Steps of Reading

IV. Practice Means Improvement

V. Foundation Skills for Life

VI. Check Your Predictions

Getting Ready to Read This Book

Reading for Success is a book that will help you improve your skills. It will help you to read better, write better, and think better. Each chapter has activities you can do to make these skills easier to learn and practice. The first example of these activities is the following Prediction Guide. When you predict, you are making a guess about what might be in a reading based on what you already know about the topic. Take a few seconds to read each statement, and consider which ones you think are true. Do this before reading any further. We will discuss why we use this technique later in the chapter.

A C T I V I T Y 1 : Prediction Guide

Which statements do you think are true?

1. Reading is easy for some people, and difficult for others.

2. If I am already a good reader and writer, I will probably not benefit from this book.

3. This book can be used by a single student or a whole class.

4. This book might be good in a geography class or a technology class.

5. Making predictions about what I read can improve my ability to read.

6. Reading a book is a good way to put a person to sleep.

7. It is a good idea to write in textbooks.

8. Reading and writing are not really very closely related.

9. Reading is very similar to playing team sports.

10. If I do not like to read, this book may change my mind.

Now that you have given some thought to how you read, please continue.

A prediction does not have to be accurate to be useful. The important thing is that it stimulates us to think about the future where we will all spend the rest of our lives.

EDWARD CORNISH,
PRESIDENT
WORLD FUTURE SOCIETY

Why Read a Book to Learn How to Read a Book?

Recently, the vice-president of a major Japanese automobile manufacturer, which had located a manufacturing facility in the United States, spoke to a group of vocational and academic teachers. In that speech, he pointed out that his company was turning down two out of every three high school graduates who were applying for work with his company. The reasons he gave for this situation were that the applicants, though high school graduates, could not read and they could not solve problems. But high school graduates are supposed to be able to read. Then what was he talking about? Look at the passage below, and see if you can answer the questions that follow.

A C T I V I T Y 2 : **The Golfer Passage**

"Do I deserve a mulligan?" asked Bob.

"No, but don't take a drop," said Al. "Use a hand-mashie, then fly the bogey high to the carpet and maybe you'll get a gimme within the leather."

"You're right," said Bob, "I'll cover the flag for a birdie and at least get a ginsberg if I'm not stymied."

1. Does Bob deserve a mulligan?
   a. Yes
   b. No
   c. Maybe

2. What does Al think Bob should do?
   a. Catch a gimme
   b. Take a drop
   c. Use a hand-mashie
   d. Fly a kite

3. What does Bob decide to do?
   a. Cover the flag
   b. Take a drop
   c. Birdie-up

4. How can Bob get a birdie?
   a. By getting stymied
   b. By getting a ginsberg
   c. By covering the flag

5. If Bob is not stymied, what will he get?
   a. A hickie
   b. A birdie
   c. A mulligan
   d. A ginsberg

Morgan, et.al. *Critical Reading/Thinking Skills for the College Student, 2nd Edition,* (1986). Dubuque, Iowa: Kendall-Hunt, pp. 2–3.

The overwhelming majority of high school students are able to answer all five of the questions correctly. There is a problem, however, when students have to think about what the passage means. What if you were asked to offer a solution to this situation: What should Bob do if he becomes "stymied"? Many high school students are unable to offer a solution because they do not know the game of golf. They can read the words by decoding the sounds of the letters, and they can pick out facts to answer the five accompanying questions. (How many times have you answered the questions at the end of a chapter of one of your textbooks just like the preceding questions, without really understanding what they mean?) Finding answers to factual comprehension questions may bring little or no understanding to your reading.

The Three Steps of Reading

Our definition of reading is **making meaning**, which is probably the opposite of what you did when reading the passage about mulligans, ginsbergs, and getting stymied. Good readers are always making meaning out of written words, and they do this by following three steps in the reading process.

1. They **prepare** themselves to read by assessing the topic and thinking about what they already know about it or how it might relate to something similar.

2. They **help themselves to understand** the meaning of the words. They do this by creating reasons to be reading. (One way to do this is by making predictions about what you are going to read, as you did in the prediction guide before reading this chapter. Hopefully, making predictions has helped you to focus your attention and make meaning out of this chapter.)

3. They **think about what they have read**. Good readers frequently pause to check their understanding of the reading and to think about what it might mean in real life. Maybe you can now pause to think about how much you use these three phases of reading and how they can help you improve your reading ability.

A C T I V I T Y 3 : Making Meaning of the Fable About a Miser

---

You are about to read Aesop's Fable about a miser. Answer these questions before you read.

1. What is a miser?

2. What good do you think might happen to a miser?

3. What bad could happen to a miser?

4. Have you ever known a miser?

---

5. If so, describe this person.

6. Have you ever said to yourself, "If I had a lot more money, I would be happy."?

7. Have you ever known a person with a lot of money who was very frugal (tight with his money)?

8. Did he or she seem like a happy person?

Help yourself to understand by paying special attention to these words as you read: **horrified**, **comforted**.

The Miser

There was once a man who loved money so much that he would not spend one cent of his money if he could help it. All the Miser did all day was look at his money, and hold it in his hands, and brag to himself about how rich he was. One day he decided to sell nearly everything he had to exchange his money for a lump of gold. But then the Miser was afraid someone would steal his new lump of gold. So he dug a hole by the wall of his garden and buried it.

Every morning he would go to his wall and dig up his treasure, to have the pleasure of looking at it. Then he would bury it again.

One morning when he was going to his hiding place he was horrified that someone had been there before him, had dug up the ground, and taken the gold.

"Thieves!" he screamed. "I have been robbed!" He began to weep and moan so loudly that his neighbor came running.

"Don't take it so hard," he comforted the Miser when he heard the story. "Nothing so bad has happened to you. Just bury a stone there and pretend that it is gold. Since you never intended to spend it, a stone will be just as good as a lump of gold."

A C T I V I T Y 4 : Learning from the Fable

It is not very important whether your answers to the questions preceding the fable were correct or not. What is important is that your answers were predictions that helped to focus on the meaning of the fable. Think now about what we can learn from this fable. On a sheet of paper list a number of things that you learned.

This book is designed to help you learn many ways to apply the three steps to good reading. We call these ways of making meaning from books **strategies**. Stop and think for a moment about your favorite sport. It may be tennis, swimming, baseball, soccer, or something else. No matter what sport it is, you probably work hard when you play it. You may run and sweat a great deal,

College of Mt. St. Joseph, Cincinnati

and you probably even suffer pain at times when you play it. Successful reading is also hard work.

If reading is hard work for you, guess what? It is the same for most people! The difference is that some people have **strategies** or action plans that they use to help them save energy and make reading easier. Would you consider playing your favorite sport without a strategy?

Just as coaches and players have strategies to be successful in sports, successful readers have strategies they use to get the most from textbooks and other written materials. The many strategies in this book will show you ways to master specific reading skills.

A C T I V I T Y 5 : Personal Inventory

Review the checklist on the next page. On a sheet of paper complete the checklist, considering which skills you feel strong in and which skills you need to improve.

Keep your checklist as a personal inventory of your reading strengths and weaknesses. As you work through the reading activities in this text, refer to your checklist as a reminder of what skills you need to improve.

	I could improve in this	I feel strong in this
1. Basic comprehension		
2. Vocabulary and word attack skills		
3. Previewing and preparing for reading		
4. Note taking		
5. Study skills		
6. Speed reading		
7. Thinking at different levels		
8. Problem solving		
9. Reading to find or check information		
10. Reading to follow directions		
11. Reading to draw conclusions		
12. Writing to improve thinking		

Practice Means Improvement

Each chapter of this text will have activities using real textbook and technical readings to allow you to practice the strategies of reading, much like the activities that you recently completed. Both in the chapters and in the end of chapter activities, you will have the chance to practice these strategies.

This text will also allow you to apply the strategies you learn to your own textbooks in whatever subjects you are taking. Just as practicing sports in real game-like conditions is very important, we think the best way to learn to apply reading strategies used in school, work and in life is to actually use your own books.

Foundation Skills for Life

Reading, writing, and thinking skills have been identified in a national survey called the SCANS Report (Secretary's Commission on Achieving Necessary Skills) as foundational skills for success in today's workplace. The skills you learn in this book can translate into lifelong success. Students who work at improving their reading and study skills enter the work world or college with an edge over students who are not strategic at reading and writing.

If most American students knew and practiced the skills you will learn in this book, perhaps two of three would not have been turned away from high-paying jobs that require reading, writing, and thinking skills.

A C T I V I T Y 6 : **Making Meaning**

Glance over the following paragraphs on time management and jot down some ideas about the topic on a separate sheet of paper. This will help you prepare to read. Now read about time management and as you read, help yourself to understand by paying special attention to these words: **distinguish**, **barriers**, **abuse**, and **procrastinate**. Ask yourself to think about what this passage identifies as the common "time wasters" that rob us of productivity in the workplace.

Time Management

You learned that time management is the process of planning your activities to gain better control over your time. Managing your time effectively is critical to your success on the job. You will want to learn how to eliminate time wasters and handle time obligations efficiently. Analyzing how you spend your time will help you become more effective in managing your work. One of the first steps in learning how to use your time is recognizing how your time can be wasted. In the office setting, you will need to learn to distinguish between time obligations and time wasters.

Common Time Wasters

Often not all time spent "at work" is productive. You can waste time without realizing it. Following are some common time wasters you may encounter, along with suggestions on overcoming them.

Unnecessary Telephone Conversations

To the office assistant, the telephone can be either a time saver or a time waster. Often, a telephone call that starts out as a time saver can become a time waster. For example, if an office worker takes ten minutes to verify information on a price list and five minutes to discuss the latest episode of a favorite television program, a conversation which started out as productive ends up being a time waster. If this happens two or three times a day, the time lost can add up rapidly.

Frequent Interruptions

Interruptions in your work can come from drop-in visitors and even your supervisor. Discouraging the drop-in visitor may involve building **barriers** against interruptions. If you have a door, close it. If possible, turn your workstation so that you do not face an open door or common passageway. If you do not need an extra chair by your workstation, remove it.

Excessive Socializing

Although some socializing will help you maintain good working relations with your coworkers, too much socialization is an **abuse** of company time. Some workers may socialize too much, and you will be wise to avoid engaging in long conversations with them. When a talker tries to involve you in idle conversation, offer a simple response like: "I really must get back to work. Maybe we could discuss this at lunch." You will maintain good working relations while excusing yourself to continue your work. If you are consistent in your responses, the talker will soon learn that you are not distracted easily from your work.

Also, be careful not to mistreat your lunch time and your break time by extending them beyond the approved time periods.

Ineffective Communication

You will be expected to follow both written and oral instructions from your supervisor and coworkers. You will also be expected to give clear written and oral instructions to others. As you learned in Chapter 3, if the information given or received is inaccurate or incomplete, much time can be lost in doing a task wrong and correcting it. Be certain the instructions and directions you give are specific and accurate. Likewise, be sure that you understand any instructions you receive.

Disorganization

Being disorganized can be a major time waster. Searching for the paper you just had in your hands, missing important deadlines, and shifting unnecessarily from one project to another are all signs of a disorganized person. Take the time to organize your work area and prepare a daily plan for your work. You should think through and thoughtfully plan complicated jobs before starting them. Group similar tasks together and avoid jumping from one project to another before finishing the first task. Do not **procrastinate**. If unpleasant or difficult tasks are left for later, they can become potential crises just waiting to erupt.

> *There is no such thing as a problem without a gift for you in its hands. You seek problems because you need their gifts.*
>
> FROM *ILLUSIONS* BY RICHARD BACH, 1977

Oliverio, M.E., Pasewark, W.R., and White, B.R. *The Office: Procedures and Technology, 2nd Ed.* (1993). Cincinnati, Ohio: South-Western Publishing, pp. 398–400. Used with permission.

ACTIVITY 7: Summarizing

The dictionary defines *summary* as a brief report covering the main points of a reading. To help you summarize, remember that you must do these operations:

- Look for the "biggest" and most important terms.
- Use the bold-faced headings to clue you in to major concepts.
- Omit any repetitions in your summary.
- Omit any unnecessary material.

With the above in mind, summarize on a sheet of paper what you learned in the reading about the difficulties of wasting time when considering time management.

Check Your Predictions

Before you go on to Chapter 2, check the predictions you made before reading the first chapter. Did you predict accurately?

1. Reading is easy for some people, and difficult for others.

2. If I am already a good reader and writer, I will probably not benefit from this book.

3. This book can be used by a single student or a whole class.

4. This book might be good in a geography class or a technology class.

5. Making predictions about what I read can improve my ability to read.

6. Reading a book is a good way to put a person to sleep.

7. It is a good idea to write in textbooks.

8. Reading and writing are not really very closely related.

9. Reading is very similar to playing team sports.

10. If I do not like to read, this book may change my mind.

More important to you, did making predictions help prepare you for what you would read? Did you find yourself reading to find out if you were correct? If so, you were *practicing strategic reading!*

1. You **prepared** yourself by thinking of the concept of reading as hard work, the similarity of reading and sports, and how to use this book.

2. You also created a personal desire to find out if you were right by checking or not checking the statements beforehand. Thus you were **helping yourself to understand** by creating the need to find out.

3. And right now you are reflecting, or **thinking about what you read** and how much you understood. Congratulations! You are a strategic reader! The remainder of this book will show you more ways to do what you did in this chapter.

SUMMARY

In this chapter, you have learned the need for new strategies for making meaning when reading, including:

- predicting before you read

- preparing to read

- helping yourself to understand the meaning of words

- thinking about what you've read

- learning that strategies are like plans to promote better reading skills

WRITER'S WORKSHOP 1

Don't worry about reading in-depth the following chapter section on "Filing Records". Simply glance over it in order to notice the reading helps that are provided to the reader. In a few sentences, write what you think is an important or primary point made in this passage. Share these with your class, compare your thoughts and discuss your answers.

> You need to set aside time each day to file. This may seem simple to do, but it is not. Many other tasks often seem more important than filing. But if the rest of your tasks are to go smoothly, the records management system cannot become **clogged** with stacks of unfiled records. If you have followed the five steps for preparing records for storage, you can file the records easily and quickly by following these procedures:
>
> 1. Locate the proper file drawer by reading the drawer labels.
>
> 2. Search through the guides in the drawer to locate the desired alphabetic or numeric section.
>
> 3. If an individual folder has been prepared for the record, place the record in the folder with the front of the record facing the front of the folder and the top of the record at the left side. You should arrange records in an individual folder according to date, with the most recent record in front.
>
> 4. If no individual folder is available, file the record in the general folder for that section. You should arrange records in a general folder alphabetically by name or subject. If there are two or more records

for the same number or subject, they are arranged according to date with the most recent record in front.

Using Special Folders

Some companies use special folders as well as general and individual folders.

A **special folder** is a type of general folder that is used for a variety of "special" purposes. For example, you may remove all the records coded **Smith** from the general folder and place them in a special folder, thus permitting material filed under **Smith** to be found more quickly. You also may prepare special folders to collect miscellaneous information about a particular subject or project, such as **ARMA Convention Travel Plans**. You arrange records alphabetically in a special folder. Within each group of names or subjects, arrange the records by date.

Avoiding Overcrowded Files

Never allow folders to become overcrowded. Usually a folder has **score lines** at the bottom. Creasing the score lines widens the folder and increases its capacity. But a folder should not contain more than an inch of filed material.

When a folder becomes too full, **subdivide** the records into two or more folders. The folder labels should accurately reflect the contents of the new folders. For example, the folders could be labeled by date or subject:

Be sure to examine general folders often so you can prepare individual and special folders when necessary. It is best not to fill a file drawer to capacity. You should have enough room in the drawer so that you can move the folders easily.

Oliverio, M.E., Pasewark, W.R., and White, B.R. *The Office: Procedures and Technology, 2nd Ed..* (1993). Cincinnati, Ohio: South-Western Publishing, pp. 553–554. Used with permission.

Make a list of the aids provided the reader to help in comprehending the text. There are as many as *four* ways that the author gives help to the readers in the passage. Think about how you used the four helps. Write out specific ways you could use these four textbook aids in studying another textbook that you are currently reading.

WRITER'S WORKSHOP 2

Read the following set of instructions from an owner's manual and installation guide for an outside door. As you read, think about what you know about doors and visualize how you would use the instructions to install the door. Then rewrite the instructions in your own words. Writing these directions in your own words will help make certain that you understand them.

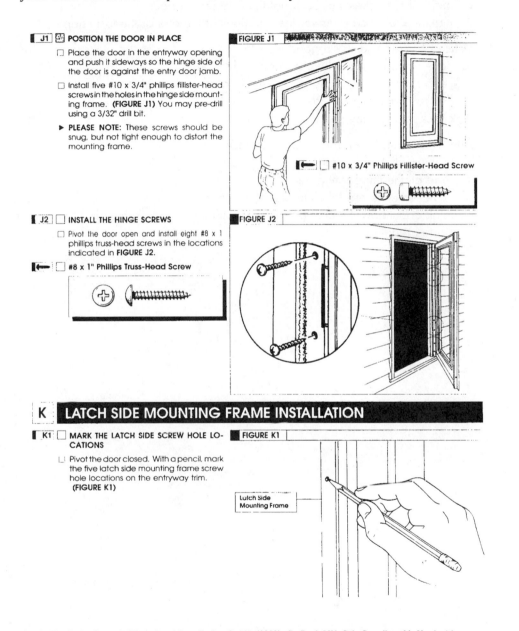

J1 ⚃ POSITION THE DOOR IN PLACE

☐ Place the door in the entryway opening and push it sideways so the hinge side of the door is against the entry door jamb.

☐ Install five #10 x 3/4" phillips fillister-head screws in the holes in the hinge side mounting frame. **(FIGURE J1)** You may pre-drill using a 3/32" drill bit.

▶ **PLEASE NOTE:** These screws should be snug, but not tight enough to distort the mounting frame.

FIGURE J1

☐ #10 x 3/4" Phillips Fillister-Head Screw

J2 ☐ INSTALL THE HINGE SCREWS

☐ Pivot the door open and install eight #8 x 1 phillips truss-head screws in the locations indicated in **FIGURE J2**.

☐ #8 x 1" Phillips Truss-Head Screw

FIGURE J2

K LATCH SIDE MOUNTING FRAME INSTALLATION

K1 ☐ MARK THE LATCH SIDE SCREW HOLE LO-CATIONS

☐ Pivot the door closed. With a pencil, mark the five latch side mounting frame screw hole locations on the entryway trim. **(FIGURE K1)**

FIGURE K1

Latch Side Mounting Frame

Cambridge Series Owner's Manual and Installation Guide, (1992). St. Paul, MN: Cole Sewell, p. 11. Used with permission.

FINAL CHECK

Answer these questions as a final check of how well you read.

1. Before beginning to read a new chapter, I always
   a. see how many pages are in the reading.
   b. look up all of the big words in the dictionary.
   c. make some guesses about what the chapter is about.
   d. make certain I can answer the questions at the end of the last chapter.

2. While I am reading, it's a good idea to
   a. have someone read the chapter aloud to me.
   b. keep track of how many pages I have read.
   c. list the chapter's main idea.
   d. check to see if my predictions are right or wrong.

3. After I have read a chapter, it's a good idea to
   a. look up all the big words in a dictionary.
   b. read all the important parts.
   c. have someone read the chapter aloud to me.
   d. think about how the chapter was like things I already knew about before I started reading.

Answers: 1. c; 2. d; 3. d

Previewing Reading Selections

CHAPTER OBJECTIVES

After completing Chapter Two, you will be able to :

- explain the importance of previewing reading materials.

- describe how to preview before you read.

- compare the differences in previewing fiction and non-fiction materials.

- explain how to become more interested in a particular reading by asking quality questions before reading.

- explain why it is important to know as much as possible about each of your textbooks and how they are organized.

Chapter Outline

I. Previewing Reading Selections

II. How to Preview

III. Using Quality Questions to Preview

IV. Asking Wild and Wacky Questions

V. Your Textbook as a Tool

OPENING ACTIVITY

Before reading, take two or three minutes to flip through the pages of this chapter, looking only at the words that stand out because they are in bold print or they are bigger than most of the words. Also take the time to look at the pictures and read the captions under each picture. After you have done this, begin reading below.

Previewing Reading Selections

Have you ever noticed that often before a TV episode of your favorite prime time program they show two or three short film clips of action from later in the show? They might be action scenes or even two people embracing or holding hands. Have you ever thought about why the producers of a show do that; or how they decide which film clips to use?

Just as you have learned, in the first chapter, to prepare yourself for reading, TV producers have learned to prepare the audience for viewing a TV episode. They know that the film will be more interesting if you know a little bit about what is to come later. You have seen just enough to know that some very interesting things are going to happen, and perhaps enough about how people will relate to one another in the film to be interested in seeing how the relationships occur or develop. The whole film makes more sense to you as you watch because of the preview. And it is easier to watch because you know something exciting or interesting is going to happen later on in the film.

Minds are like parachutes. They only function when they are open.

SIR JAMES DEWAR

Previewing Is Pre-reading

When you are getting ready to read, you can use the same technique to make readings more interesting and understandable. Read the following passage in Activity 1, and answer the accompanying questions.

A C T I V I T Y 1 : The Worried Man

The man was worried. His car came to a halt and he was all alone. It was extremely dark and cold. The man took off his overcoat, rolled down the window, and got out of the car as quickly as possible. Then he used all his strength to move as fast as he could. He was relieved when he finally saw the lights of the city, even though they were far away.

Kiewra, Kenneth A. "An Embedded Curriculum Approach For Teaching Students How To Learn", *Home School Collaboration, Enhancing Children's Academic and Social Competence*, (1993). Sandra L. Christenson and Jane Close, Eds., National Association of School Psychologists, Silver Spring, Md.

1. Did you understand what happened in the passage? What the man did?

2. Why did the man take off his overcoat?

3. Why did the man roll down the window?

Did you understand the passage? Most people would say that they do understand it, but if you were asked why the man took off his overcoat, or why he rolled down the window, how would you respond? What if, before you had read it, you saw a picture of the scene and it showed a car under water in a river? If you had known ahead of time that the passage was about a car submerged in water, would those questions have been easier to answer? Would you have understood the passage better the first time?

Having a clue about what you are reading can make reading easier to do and more enjoyable. Just as "The Worried Man" passage is easier to understand when we know it is about a submerged car, your textbook readings for school can be easier for you once you learn how to preview your reading. Everything will make more sense to you and studying will be easier.

Asking Questions When Previewing

Previewing a chapter takes very little time. Some of the questions you should answer for yourself when you preview are:

- How interested am I in this selection?

- How much do I already know about this topic?

- How deeply do I need to think and concentrate to learn this material?

- How fast can I read this material?

- What do I still need to learn about this topic?

Planning Your Strategy

When you ask such questions you are helping yourself to understand the reading. At the same time you are "scouting" the material to see how to plan your reading. Just as you would plan carefully to have on hand the ingredients necessary for a recipe to make chocolate chip cookies, when you preview, you are planning carefully by analyzing the reading selection and preparing your strategy for that material.

Sometimes the preview gives you all the information you need, and consequently you don't even have to read it! But in many instances the preview will build anticipation for material that is not familiar to you.

Seeing Your Results

In an informal study with a group of high school science and geography students, some of the students were asked to read a selection without using previewing strategies, while the other students conducted a preview before reading. Both sets of students were asked ten comprehension questions after their reading. The group that didn't use the previewing strategy answered 20 percent fewer questions correctly. The preview strategy significantly helped the group's comprehension of the selection. Such a strategy, if you practice it carefully, should improve your reading comprehension, too. In addition, it will make the reading more interesting since you will know in advance what it will be about and how difficult it will be for you to read. Then you can have a useful **strategy** for reading!

How to Preview

The reason that previewing can improve your understanding of a reading is that it can help you clarify your thinking about the subject of the reading and what you might learn from the text. Also you will know how much effort you will need to put into the task, allowing you to accomplish the following:

1. gain confidence

2. read in a more relaxed way

3. be more interested

4. feel better about the material

In addition, previewing strategies help you determine how much you already know about the subject because of your own background and experience. The result is that you are clearer about what you know and what you need to know. In a way, it makes you want to read before you have begun.

What to Look For

When previewing a textbook reading or other technical reading, you should examine and think about the following:

- Title and Subtitle—These will tell you the overall topic of the chapter or article.

- Introduction—This may be a section headed "Introduction" or only a paragraph with no heading. It tells you what the author intends to talk about.

- Headings and Sub-headings—Each heading is the topic for that section. Forming these headings into questions gives purpose to the reading.

- Graphs, Charts, Maps, Tables, Pictures—Interpreting these before reading will help you to understand the chapter or article when you read.

- **Bold Print** and *Italicized Words*—These are obviously important to notice!

- Summary—This may be a section titled "Summary" or "Conclusion" or a final paragraph. It might be at the end of the reading or at the end of the chapter. You need to know the structure of your own textbook so you can find the summary easily. (Even though it is usually located at the end of each section or chapter, you should read this **before** reading the text.)

- Questions—Review any post-passage questions. They point out topics of importance to be covered in the chapter.

Making Decisions

After the preview described above you will be ready to decide:

- what you already know about the material based on your background of experience and the preview itself, and

- what you need to learn in reading the material.

You can then turn those things that are not known into questions to give you reasons for reading. Once you have done this you have made your job much easier!

Previewing Fiction

When reading fictional stories or novels, the preview procedure is slightly different. You need to look at

- the title

- the introduction

- the pictures

Then, it is necessary to stop from time to time and make guesses about the outcome of the story or what is going to happen next. This heightens suspense and helps hold your interest. More important, it gives you purpose for reading; namely to find out whether or not your predictions were right. By doing this when you read fiction, you help yourself to understand the story better. This type of reading will be discussed in more detail in Chapter Four.

Preparing to Read Technical Materials

Of all materials, students probably have the least experience with reading technical textbooks and workplace manuals. Such texts require you to **think critically** about the contents; that is, to figure out how several pieces of information are related. Often, technical reading requires you to solve a problem. Finally, thinking critically means that you must decide how the material might relate to a specific situation or personal experience.

A C T I V I T Y 2 : Previewing Practice

You may use the selection that follows on engine cooling systems, one of the additional readings in the Appendix of this textbook, or use your own textbook in any non-fiction or technical subject area to complete this practice exercise. The marginal notes (in black) show what you should look for when previewing, and the possible thoughts (in color) of an imaginary reader who is previewing that reading. By reading the thoughts in color, in the margin, you can get an idea of some of the things that might go through the mind of a reader preparing to read this. Use these questions to help you as you are previewing:

1. How interested am I in the selection?

2. How much do I already know about the topic?

3. How much do I need to concentrate and think to learn this material?

4. How fast can I read this material?

5. What do I still need to learn about this topic?

Make certain you remember and look for the following as you preview:

- Title
- Subtitle
- Introduction
- Headings
- Sub-headings
- Bold Print and Italics
- Pictures (Be sure to read the captions with each one, and study the picture to think about why the author used that picture to illustrate meaning.)
- Graphs, Maps, Charts, Tables
- Summary
- Review Questions

After previewing, rephrase the headings and sub-headings into questions and record them on a sheet of paper. (For instance, if you were previewing this chapter of this book, and you saw the chapter subtitle, PREVIEWING FICTION, you might write down the question, "How do you preview fiction?") After you have finished a preview and written questions, read the entire selection to find answers to your questions. Then note your answers on your paper. What you will have discovered is that previewing definitely helps make you more interested in what you are reading.

Unit 6 Cooling Systems

I wonder what a water jacket does?

OBJECTIVES   After completing this unit, the student should be able to:
- Discuss the construction of the water jacket and trace the path of cooling water through the engine.
- Explain the construction and operation of the water pump and trace the path of water through the pump.
- List the basic parts of the air-cooling system and trace the path of cooling air through the engine.

My uncle replaced the water pump in his car.

Wow! I never knew that!

INTRODUCTION

In internal combustion engines, the temperature of combustion often reaches over 4000° Fahrenheit, a temperature well beyond the melting point of the engine parts. This intense heat cannot be allowed to build up. A carefully engineered cooling system is, therefore, a vital part of every engine. A cooling system must maintain a good engine operating temperature without allowing destructive heat to build up and cause engine part failure, figure 6-1.

The cooling system does not have to dispose of all the heat produced by combustion. A good portion of the heat energy is converted into mechanical energy by the engine, benefiting engine efficiency. Some heat is lost in the form of hot exhaust gases. The cooling system must dissipate about one-third of the heat energy caused by combustion.

Engines are either air-cooled or water-cooled; both systems are in common use. Generally, air-cooled engines are used to power machinery, lawn mowers, garden tractors, chain saws, etc. The air-cooled system is usually lighter in weight and simpler;

hence, its popularity for portable equipment, figure 6-2.

The water-cooled engine is often used for permanent installation or stationary power plants. Most automobile engines and outboard motors are water-cooled.

AIR-COOLING SYSTEM   ◀—— *MAIN HEADING*

The air-cooling system consists of heat radiating fins, flywheel blower, and shrouds for channeling the air. The path of airflow can be seen in figure 6-3.

Heat radiating fins are located on the cylinder head and cylinder because the greatest concentration of heat is in this area. The fins increase the heat radiating surface of these parts allowing the heat to be carried away to the atmosphere more quickly, figure 6-4.

The flywheel blower consists of air vanes cast as a part of the flywheel. As the flywheel revolves, these vanes blow cool air across the fins carrying away the heated air and replacing it with cool air.

My friend has a VW that has an air-cooled motor.

I've heard the word flywheel before, but I thought it was related to the transmission!

MAKE NOTE OF NEW WORDS

MAKE SENSE OF PICTURES BEFORE READING.

I always wondered why they had the things stick out.

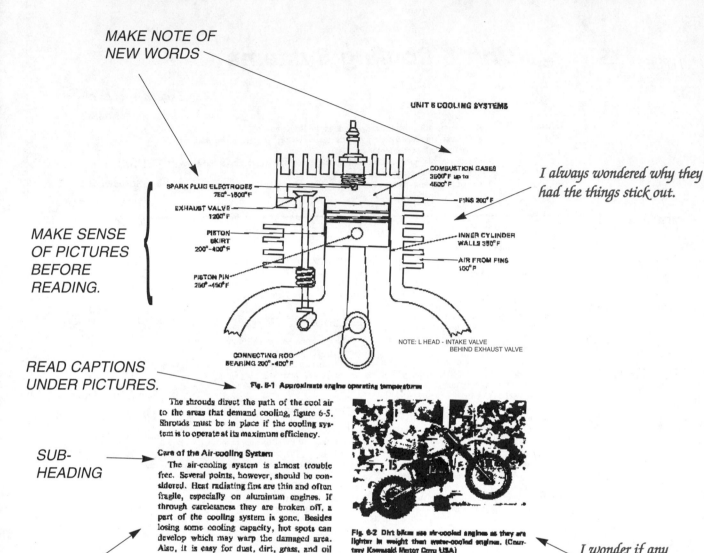

UNIT 6 COOLING SYSTEMS

SPARK PLUG ELECTRODES 750°-1500°F

EXHAUST VALVE 1200°F

PISTON SKIRT 200°-400°F

PISTON PIN 250°-450°F

COMBUSTION GASES 3500°F up to 4500°F

FINS 200°F

INNER CYLINDER WALLS 350°F

AIR FROM FINS 100°F

NOTE: L HEAD - INTAKE VALVE BEHIND EXHAUST VALVE

CONNECTING ROD BEARING 200°-400°F

READ CAPTIONS UNDER PICTURES.

Fig. 6-1 Approximate engine operating temperatures

The shrouds direct the path of the cool air to the areas that demand cooling, figure 6-5. Shrouds must be in place if the cooling system is to operate at its maximum efficiency.

Care of the Air-cooling System

SUB-HEADING

The air-cooling system is almost trouble free. Several points, however, should be considered. Heat radiating fins are thin and often fragile, especially on aluminum engines. If through carelessness they are broken off, a part of the cooling system is gone. Besides losing some cooling capacity, hot spots can develop which may warp the damaged area. Also, it is easy for dust, dirt, grass, and oil

Fig. 6-2 Dirt bikes use air-cooled engines as they are lighter in weight than water-cooled engines. (Courtesy Kawasaki Motor Corp USA)

Do air cooled engines work at low temperatures when they are not moving?

I wonder if any motorcycles use a water-cooled engine?

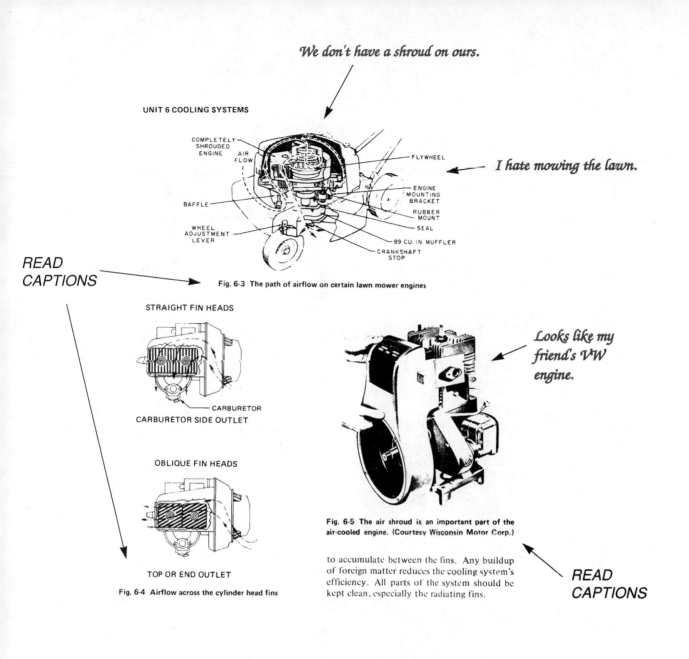

We don't have a shroud on ours.

UNIT 6 COOLING SYSTEMS

COMPLETELY
SHROUDED
ENGINE   AIR
         FLOW

FLYWHEEL

I hate mowing the lawn.

ENGINE
MOUNTING
BRACKET

RUBBER
MOUNT

BAFFLE

SEAL

WHEEL
ADJUSTMENT
LEVER

89 CU. IN. MUFFLER

CRANKSHAFT
STOP

READ CAPTIONS

Fig. 6-3 The path of airflow on certain lawn mower engines

STRAIGHT FIN HEADS

CARBURETOR
CARBURETOR SIDE OUTLET

OBLIQUE FIN HEADS

TOP OR END OUTLET

Fig. 6-4 Airflow across the cylinder head fins

Looks like my friend's VW engine.

Fig. 6-5 The air shroud is an important part of the air-cooled engine. (Courtesy Wisconsin Motor Corp.)

to accumulate between the fins. Any buildup of foreign matter reduces the cooling system's efficiency. All parts of the system should be kept clean, especially the radiating fins.

READ CAPTIONS

The flywheel vanes should not be chipped or broken. Besides reducing the cooling capacity of the engine, such damage can destroy the balance of the flywheel. An unbalanced flywheel causes vibration and an excessive amount of wear on engine parts.

MAIN HEADING

WATER-COOLING SYSTEM

Some small engines are water-cooled as are most larger engines. Such engines have an enclosed water jacket around the cylinder walls and cylinder head. Water jackets are relatively trouble free. However, damaging deposits can build up over a period of time. Salt corrosion, scale, lime, and silt can restrict the flow of water and heat transfer. Water jackets are found on most outboard motors and on the majority of automobile engines. Cool water is circulated through this jacket picking up the heat and carrying it away.

Figure 6-6 shows a cross section of water passage in the head and block. Water cooling

systems often found on stationary small gas engines or automobile engines include the following basic parts: radiator, fan, thermostat, water pump, hoses, and water jacket.

The water pump circulates the water throughout the entire cooling system. The hot water from the combustion area is carried from the engine block and head to the radiator. In the radiator, many small tubes and radiating fins dissipate the heat into the atmosphere. A fan blows cooling air over the radiating fins. From the bottom of the radiator the cool water is returned to the engine.

Engines are designed to operate with a water temperature of between 160 degrees and 180 degrees Fahrenheit. To maintain the correct water temperature a thermostat is used in the cooling system. When the temperature is below the thermostat setting, the thermostat remains closed and the cooling water circulates only through the engine, figure 6-7A. However, as the heat builds up to the thermostat setting, the thermostat opens and the cooling water moves throughout the entire system, figure 6-7B.

I wonder if water ever leaks into the cylinders?

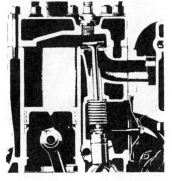

Fig. 6-6 Cross section showing water passages in head and block

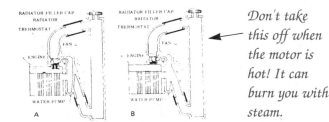

Fig. 6-7 (A) Thermostat closed: water recirculated through engine only. (B) Thermostat open: water circulated through both engine and radiator.

Don't take this off when the motor is hot! It can burn you with steam.

CAPTIONS

I love to go fishing!

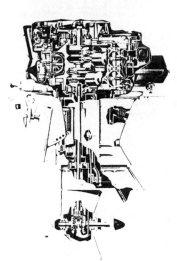

Fig. 6-8 Cutaway of an outboard motor (Courtesy Johnson Motors)

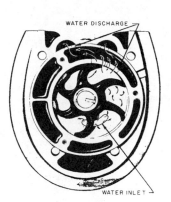

Fig. 6-10 An impeller water pump with the cover removed to show the impeller

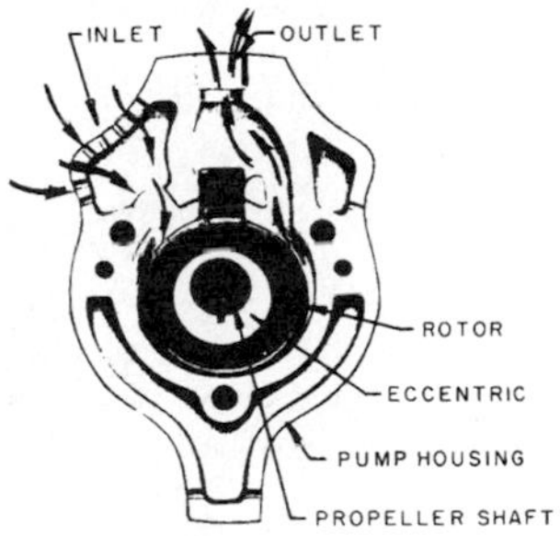

INLET   OUTLET

ROTOR
ECCENTRIC
PUMP HOUSING
PROPELLER SHAFT

Fig. 6-9 An eccentric rotor water pump with the cover removed to show the eccentric and rotor

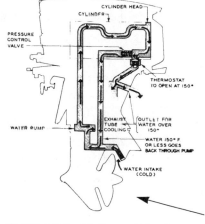

Fig. 6 11 A thermostatically controlled cooling system used on outboard engines

I never thought about how the outboard motor cools.

Wonder what happens when this gets clogged with mud or seaweed?

MAIN HEADING⟶

WATER COOLING THE OUTBOARD ENGINE

Cooling the outboard engine with water is a simpler process because there is an inexhaustible supply of cool water present where the engine operates. Outboards pump water from the source through the engine's water jacket and then discharge the water back into the source. A cutaway of an outboard motor is shown in figure 6-8.

The water pump on outboards is located in the lower unit. It is driven by the main driveshaft or the propeller shaft. The cool water is pumped up copper-tube passages to the water jacket. After the cooling water picks up heat, it is discharged into the exhaust area of the lower unit and out of the engine. Several types of water pumps are used on outboard motors. Plunger type pumps; eccentric rotor pumps, figure 6-9; and impeller pumps, figure 6-10, are some examples.

Many outboard motors, especially large horsepower models, are equipped with a thermostatically controlled cooling system, figure 6-11. The temperature of the water circulating through the water jacket is maintained at about 150° Fahrenheit.

REVIEW QUESTIONS

READ THESE BEFORE READING THE CHAPTER TO KNOW WHAT SOME IMPORTANT IDEAS ARE.

1. How high can the temperature of combustion reach?

2. Does the cooling system remove all the heat of combustion? Explain.

3. Why are air-cooling systems often used for portable equipment?

4. What are the main parts of the air-cooling system?

5. Why are cylinders and cylinder heads equipped with fins instead of being cast with a smooth surface?

6. What are the basic parts of the water-cooling system found on stationary small gas engines?

7. What is the function of the thermostat?

8. What are several types of water pumps used on outboard motors?

I can answer many of these after only previewing!

Stephenson, George E. *Power Technology*, (1986). Albany, New York: Delmar, p. 82-87.

Using Quality Questions to Preview

One way to make reading even more interesting is to make your questions more interesting. Most textbooks seem to ask questions that are at a very **literal** level of understanding. Literal level questions focus only on facts that are actually mentioned in the reading material. For example, a question found in a science textbook might ask a reader what causes acid rain to be so evident in the northeastern United States? There is good reason to want to know the answers to such questions since they help you to understand the causes and effects of acid rain.

But you can also make reading more interesting by sometimes asking questions at a higher level than those that require literal, word for word, recall of the text. And, since *YOU* are the one asking the questions, why not ask more interesting questions? Instead of just reading the words on the page, think about what the author actually meant when he wrote the text. Sometimes you have to interpret how the reading applies in the real world. For instance, when reading about acid rain, you might ask questions like:

● how would you assess the level of acid rain in a specific area?

● or how would you design a solution to the main cause of acid rain?

When you ask questions like these before reading, the reading takes on more meaning to you. It gets to be more interesting! We will discuss this more in Chapter Six.

Asking Wild and Wacky Questions

If you want reading to be even *more* interesting, try asking even *more interesting* questions! Here is how. Do not let yourself be limited by the ordinary. Ask crazy questions that seem, on the surface, to be ridiculous. For example, when studying acid rain, ask questions like, "What would Superman do to solve the problem of acid rain?"

By asking such outlandish questions you take the subject out of the ordinary level of thinking into the hypothetical level. This allows your mind to manipulate the subject matter and think about it in different ways. Even though this may seem bizarre, it can actually help you break out of limiting your ways of thinking about what you are reading, and it helps you to understand better.

When a student actually came up with the question about Superman when studying acid rain, it helped the class understand one possible solution being used to neutralize acid lakes and soil by the aerial spreading of calcium carbonate. The student's answer to the question was that Superman would take a huge container of calcium carbonate and fly high over the northeast part of the United States and spin rapidly to disperse the substance over the whole affected part of the country! Even though this may seem outlandish, it helped the students reading the science textbook to make sense out of what could have been a dry topic. The next time you use the previewing process, when it comes time to write down your questions, ask some "wild and wacky" questions and see how much more fun, interesting, and useful your reading can become.

A C T I V I T Y 3: Practice with Wild and Wacky Questions

Place this page on a copy machine to make bookmarks like the one to the right. Then you can keep one in each of your books. Doing this will help you ask better questions while you preview. Try it right now with the excerpt that follows. It is entitled "The Future Job Market." Preview it, and then use the "Question Mark" bookmark to write down some really interesting and unusual questions. Then read to find the answers to your questions. You will see how it helps in understanding the text.

QUESTION MARK

QUESTIONING FOR QUALITY THINKING

Knowledge—Identification and recall of information
   Who, what, when, where, how _____?
      Describe _____

Comprehension—Organization and selection of facts and ideas
   Retell _____ in your own words.
   What is the main idea of _____?

Application—Use of facts, rules, principles
   How is _____ an example of _____?
   How is _____ related to_____?
   Why is _____ significant?

Analysis—Separation of a whole into component parts
   What are the parts or features of _____?
   Classify _____ according to _____.
   Outline/diagram/web _____.
   How does _____ compare/contrast with _____?
   What evidence can you list for _____?

Synthesis—Combination of ideas to form a new whole
   What would you predict/infer from _____?
   What ideas can you add to _____?
   How would you create/design a new _____?
   What might happen if you combined _____
      with _____?
   What solutions would you suggest for _____?

Evaluation—Development of opinions, judgments, or decisions
   Do you agree _____?
   What do you think about_____?
   What is the most important_____?
   Prioritize_____.
   How would you decide about _____?
   What criteria would you use to assess _____?

THE FUTURE JOB MARKET

Given the factors that affect jobs, is it possible to look ahead and determine which jobs will be needed in the future? This is not a simple task. Some of the factors that affect jobs are difficult to predict. However, there are certain actions every person can take to be successfully employed in our economy.

Planning a Career

Because your employment will have an impact on nearly every aspect of your life, the choice of a career is a very important decision. Your ability to obtain and maintain employment will depend on various career planning skills. As you will learn in Chapter 12, career success will be the result of:

- Knowing your personal interests and talents.
- Exploring different types of careers.
- Assessing the changing job market.
- Obtaining skills and knowledge to fulfill the requirements of the career you desire.

People who do not give career planning careful thought often spend years in unsuitable employment. When they discover their mistake, they may find it difficult, if not impossible, to change careers.

Assessing Job Opportunities

An important part of your career planning activities is knowing in which specific job areas there will be future needs. Estimates of the need for workers in any particular job category are based upon two major factors: (1) the number of new jobs to be created, and (2) the number of people who will be replaced because of transfers and separations. Certain career areas such as health care, financial services, data processing, and retailing are expected to grow faster than the average for our economy. Other employment fields such as communications, manufacturing, and agriculture will have slower growth.

The best way to keep informed on careers with strong future opportunities is to conduct personal research. By reading newspaper and magazine articles you will learn about our changing job market and the demand for certain types of employment. Television and radio news reports on business and economic conditions can provide additional knowledge about current and future job opportunities. This information can help you select a career field that not only will be interesting but also will provide strong economic security for your future.

Continuing Education

Many research studies reveal that employers look for people who have a good general education and who have been trained in some technical area. Technological developments, competition in our economy, and the desire to make a reasonable profit require that businesses employ people who can perform their job tasks well. Increased education and advanced training will serve the needs of business as well as help you secure employment.

Daughtrey, Anne Scott. *Introduction To Business: The Economy and You,* (1992). Cincinnati: South-Western.

Your Textbook as a Tool

You are a professional. Whether you know it or not, you are a professional student. Even though you may have another job, the most important one in your life right now is being a student. The pay for doing a good job now will be coming in for the rest of your life!

Just as a carpenter's profession deals with woodworking and an artist's profession with paints or clay, your main occupation while in high school is to learn not only the subject matter of the courses you are taking, but also how to best accomplish the task of learning. And just as a carpenter and a painter must learn to be experts with the tools of their trades, you should learn to be an expert with the tools of your trade. Those tools are the things that help you to learn successfully including:

- your class notes
- your textbook
- worksheets
- audio-visual materials
- teachers
- fellow students

One of your most important tools is a textbook. Each is somewhat different from the others. Because every texbook is written in a slightly different style, the process of previewing and questioning will be different for each. Some have summary statements at the end of each subsection. In some, you

need to go to the end of the whole chapter to find the summary for each sub-section. Some don't even have summaries. Because each is different, get to know the organization of each of your textbooks. Then, when it is time to preview, you will have a ***strategy for success***.

SUMMARY

Previewing is a key to better understanding as you read. When you preview, look for the

- title and subtitle
- introduction
- headings and subheadings
- graphs, charts, maps, tables, pictures
- bold print and italicized words
- summary
- questions

A central part of previewing is asking "quality" questions that stress higher levels of thought. Readings become more interesting when you ask even more creative, wild and wacky, previewing questions. Your textbook is a tool for greater success in school. Each of your textbooks is unique. Each has its own format, which you should get to know so that you can get the most from it. From here on, be sure to preview each chapter of this book, and all your other textbooks, before you read them.

WRITER'S WORKSHOP

Using any of your current textbooks, write a plan for success by telling how you are going to make beter use of your:

- class notes
- textbook
- worksheets
- audio-visual materials
- teachers
- fellow students

to improve your study habits and study skills. Also outline the organizational plan of the textbook, telling in your own words how you think it is organized.

FINAL CHECK

Answer these questions as a final check of your understanding of this chapter.

1. Before I begin reading, it is a good idea to
   a. ask someone to read the chapter to me.
   b. read the title to see what the chapter is about.
   c. check to see if most of the words have long or short vowels in them.
   d. check to see that the pictures are in order and make sense.

2. Before I begin reading, it is a good idea to
   a. check to see that no pages are missing.
   b. make a list of the words I am not sure about.
   c. use the title and pictures to help me guess what it will be about.
   d. read the last sentence so I will know how the chapter ends.

3. Before I begin reading, it is a good idea to
   a. check to see if I have read the chapter before.
   b. use my questions and guesses as a reason to read the chapter.
   c. make sure I can pronounce all the words before I start.
   d. think of a better title for the chapter.

Answers: 1. b; 2. c; 3. b

Getting the Most Out of Your Reading

CHAPTER 3

CHAPTER OBJECTIVES

This chapter will help you get the most out of your reading by showing ways to think about what you read, to connect what you read to what you know and to use writing to clarify your reading. After completing Chapter Three, you will be able to:

- prepare better before reading.

- connect and apply what you read.

- check on your understanding.

- clarify your thinking.

Chapter Outline

I. Preparing to Make Meaning of Your Reading

II. Making Connections and Applications

III. Checking What You Understand

IV. Using Writing to Clarify Your Thinking

OPENING ACTIVITY

Take the time to preview this chapter. Make certain you study:

- title

- introduction

- chapter sub-titles

- quotes highlighted throughout the chapter

- any boldfaced print

- pictures

- summary

- review questions

Preparing to Make Meaning of Your Reading

Lewis Carroll's quote lets us laugh at our ability to believe a lot of things that we know are impossible. But as readers, writers, and especially thinkers, allowing possibilities of thought leads to understanding and truth.

Preparing yourself to read by doing a pre-reading activity gets you involved with the words in the reading. It allows you to consider a variety of possibilities. If you take a little time to prepare, you'll be able to gain more meaning from your reading.

When you look through a passage or selected text, read and choose words you already know that you think are important for understanding the reading selection. You can list and define the unknown words later. It's important for you to begin with the words you do know, so you can prepare yourself to accept what the text offers. *Making your own meaning* from reading is easy to do:

1. Preview important selected words in piece of reading.

2. Make a written or mental list of those words.

3. Think about what the words suggest.

4. Decide on what they mean to you.

At times, you do these steps unconsciously, but you should get into the habit of going through these quick steps when you are about to read something important, something unfamiliar or something for a specific purpose other than pleasure reading.

More than anything you can do *after* reading, this preparation activity will increase your ability to make meaning, to understand and to remember what you've read.

> *Sometimes I've believed as many as six impossible things before breakfast.*
>
> LEWIS CAROLL

A C T I V I T Y 1 : Word Find

Don't read the passage: "In His Own League." Follow the 4 steps outlined earlier:

1. Preview selected words in the piece of reading.

2. List these key words.

3. Think about what the words suggest.

4. Decide on what they mean to you.

Look through the passage and **list** approximately **10** words that you think might be important in this reading. (You should omit words like *and, an, a, the, etc.*)

Look at your list of words and think about what these words mean as you do the following:

1. Group words that, for any reason, are alike.

2. Connect words that seem related.

3. Mark words that seem positive (+) or negative (–).

4. Write down a connected idea, a person, a place or an object related to a word or group of words.

5. Cross out some words and replace them with other words from the passage that have a stronger connection for you.

6. Circle the three "most important" words in your list.

Share your word list in pairs or small groups. **Look at, listen to** and **think about** what other students did with their word lists. Keep an open mind and be alert as you discuss.

Now **read** the passage silently or aloud.

In His Own League

As a boy, I played baseball in Columbus Park with the other boys in my neighborhood. We were of varied ages and abilities. We played from right after breakfast, sometimes took a break for lunch, and then played until dinner. On some long summer days, we met after dinner to play again until the street lamps and swarms of moths warned us that it was getting late. The next day the schedule was the same. We never practiced, never had uniforms and never made the playoffs; what we did do was have a lot of fun and truly play the game. Everyone played—we had no subs—and uneven sides meant that the team with the extra man usually did something to make it fair: one less strike, one less out or one less foul ball.

One special neighborhood player I remember, Ricky, was a handicapped kid who played every day. He had a deformed arm and hand, and he wore a metal brace on his left leg. Ricky could pitch, catch and hit one-handed shots without our help. Ricky labored when he ran the bases after a hit, so when we didn't *need* an out or it was close at first after a hop to the shortstop, we *let* him be safe. He wasn't the fastest player or slickest fielder, but he always played. He kept his mitt tucked under his bad arm when he pitched and slipped it on when he needed to catch. After a catch, he'd deftly reverse the process. He managed pretty well, and he always got picked to play. You see, we never thought of him as anything else but another kid who wanted to play baseball. Sometimes at bat he caught the ball just right with his one-arm lash and sent it for a ride into the outfield; even the longest drive meant only a double for Ricky, but he was happy. I can still picture his wide grin as he turned his head quickly from side to side just to make sure he really had made it safe to second and to let us know he was a threat to score.

Now that you've read the passage, review your word list "work sheet." Can you see the passage in a new way? Can you begin to make a more complete meaning? Write one *meaningful comment* or *interesting connection* that your word list or one from your group has with this passage. Write one *change in your thinking* that reading the passage caused.

Even though this passage *is* about a boy playing baseball, it has more meaning than that. Did your word list, your discussion and your reading show this?

Preparing to read seems like a long process. It does take time to go through the steps when you are learning how. You'll increase your speed and ease with this **word find technique** the more you apply it. Eventually, you may choose to do the process mentally or in the margin of the reading, if it's some material you can write on. The **Word Find** activity gets you involved with the text. You can use this technique for any piece of reading, long or short: a news article, a passage in a history textbook, a chapter opening in a novel or a passage on a reading comprehension test. It works best when the reason you're reading is to get a complete understanding of the text.

Why should you take the time to do this suggested activity? Athletes warm up by going through a routine of particular movements (throwing, kicking, moving) before they play. Musicians get ready to perform their song by playing a series of specific, related notes. In the same way, a reader does a similar kind of reading "warm-up" to perform the task of reading and understanding.

> "*Learning without thought is labor lost.*"
>
> CONFUCIUS

Making Connections and Applications

Reading for meaning that you can **use** and **remember** is hard work. For this labor to pay off, you need to think in very focused ways about your reading. Good readers make meaning for themselves by **connecting** what they read to what they know, what they've experienced or what they've heard. When readers are confused or stumped by what they read, often it's because they can't make these connections. While there are no absolute ways to understand something with which you are totally unfamiliar, there are some helpful things you can do. Try Activity 2 to practice connecting and applying what you read.

A C T I V I T Y   2 : Plug In Connections

Review the travel advertisement on the next page and read the paragraph. Use it as a model/example for Activity 2.

Connect or apply what you've read to what you know:

1. Connect one specific bit of the reading to something you do know about.
   (example: You know that deserts are dry and hot.)

2. Personalize the reading.

   (example: If you've seen a picture, poster, or video of the Grand Canyon, write what you remember.)

3. Apply the reading to your world.

   (example: Think about how hot the sun makes you feel in July. Imagine how much hotter it might be in the desert.)

4. Form an opinion.

   (example: A desert would be an unusual place to go for a vacation.)

5. Focus on something you need to know.
   (example: Why is this desert in Arizona called the "Painted Desert?")

This paragraph about Arizona can be more interesting, easier to understand and easier to remember if you *interact* with it in some of the ways suggested. Let your imagination and thinking assist you in making meaning.

Choose a passage from your class textbook or reading and apply the 5 **Plug in Connection** steps to it. Write your own examples for each specific step to show how you've personally connected with the text.

> *People are usually more convinced by reasons they discover themselves than those found by others.*
>
> BLAISE PASCAL

Checking What You Understand

Sherlock Holmes, the great fictional detective, solved most of his cases by carefully going over the "known" clues in his mind. He told his assistant, Dr. Watson, who complained that looking at clues in a mystery made it *more* confusing, that, "On the contrary, I only require a few missing links to have an entirely connected case."

Sherlock Holmes gives *readers* good advice. Good readers look at words they read like detectives look at clues. While the clues at first may seem confusing, they become more clear as you look at them closely. Words can sometimes mean what a reader wants them to mean and not what the writer intended. That's why **sharing** is an absolutely necessary step in fully understanding something! Good readers make meaning for themselves by linking the words they read, but they are *open* to what others may think, too. Being able to see a variety of meanings is a big step towards understanding.

Sherlock Holmes does three simple but effective things to solve every mystery:

- He **observes carefully**.

- He **thinks thoroughly**.

- He **connects clues**.

He uses no other high-tech equipment or special devices except his mind. Holmes considers **details** important and **reviews** them often. When Holmes is unfamiliar with something, he asks about it. Even with his sharp mind, he knows how necessary it is to ask the right questions. Readers who want to make meaning of what they read should follow his example.

One way to take what Sherlock Holmes does best as a master detective and apply it to your reading is to examine words, phrases and lines that stand out in a piece of reading. In the next two activities, you can practice this technique.

Triangle Truths

Triangle truths will increase your overall understanding of what you read by letting you focus on some important details. **Triangle truths** are actual triangles you draw that contain four important pieces of information. One piece of information goes at each corner of the triangle (the clues), and one piece (the response) that a reader must supply goes in the center of the triangle. All the bits of information are connected to define, describe or highlight a particular idea, person or fact from your reading. The goal in this activity is to supply the correct response to the question in the center of the triangle. To do this, readers have to check the reading and their understanding.

Triangle truths, eventually, should be designed by you after you've read a particular passage. You should share these with classmates who have read the same material. By trading triangles with others and working through them, you become familiar with key points that exist in whatever you're reading.

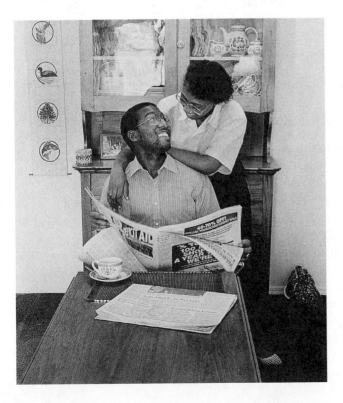

Look at the following practice **triangle truths** and supply the answers to the questions in the center. These triangles are designed to tap your general knowledge and do not refer directly to any selected piece of reading.

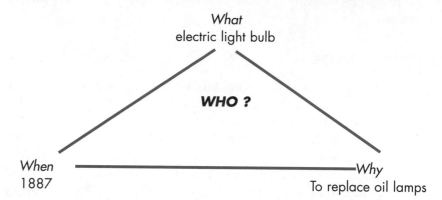

What
electric light bulb

WHO ?

When
1887

Why
To replace oil lamps

Did you come up with the famous American inventor of the light bulb? Try another practice *triangle truth*.

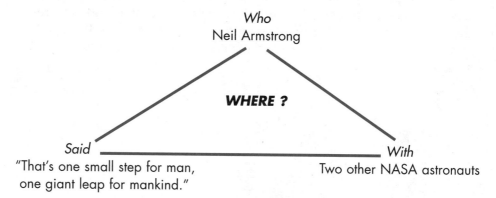

Who
Neil Armstrong

WHERE ?

Said
"That's one small step for man,
one giant leap for mankind."

With
Two other NASA astronauts

Did you come up with the location of this history-making landing?

Without reading the actual passages where this information might be found and using only your general knowledge, it's safe to assume that you would identify the "Who?" as **Thomas A. Edison**, and the "Where?" as **the moon**! This information may have been found in readings from a science or history textbook. Of course, the difficulty of these **triangle truths** depends on the reading material and details you choose to highlight.

To create these triangles, you need to refer to the text for specific information. You can be creative in what bits of information you provide and what response you hope a reader will supply. As a triangle creator, looking over a passage to design your own helps *you* remember its details. As a triangle solver, looking through a passage for the correct response to complete a triangle designed by a classmate gives you the opportunity to review useful information as you search. This activity can help you zero in on the important details found in a text and make them stick in your memory.

A C T I V I T Y 4: **More Triangle Truths**

Practice a triangle truth designed from the information taken from an actual passage. Read the following passage and supply the correct response to the triangle that follows:

St. Petersburg, Russia

Formerly called Leningrad, *Sankt Peterburg*, is a city on the delta of the Neva River, at the eastern end of the Gulf of Finland. The city is built on both banks of the Neva and on islands in the river. It is the second largest city in Russia and a major seaport. St. Petersburg is famous for its elaborate palaces, museums and cathedrals. One of the city's most visited attractions is the Winter Palace on the bank of the Neva River. It was the winter home of the czars before the 1917 Russian Revolution. Today it houses one of the greatest art collections in the world in its museum, The Hermitage. Visitors to St. Petersburg admire its alluring beauty and rich history.

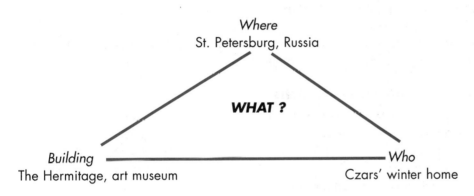

Where
St. Petersburg, Russia

WHAT ?

Building
The Hermitage, art museum

Who
Czars' winter home

Did you search the text to find one of the "most visited attractions" in this city? The correct response is the "Winter Palace." Use the same passage about the city of St. Petersburg to construct your *own* triangle. Focus on a detail that you think is important from the reading. There are no absolute rules for exactly what word should be at each corner of the triangle. Your choices for the corners and center should be your own. You can use almost any appropriate word for each of the four categories: **who, what, where, when, how, why, said, did, with, tried, wanted, made, found, etc.**

Triangle truths can apply to all subjects. Consider using them for concepts in science, math, foreign language, technology and any other subject that involves reading. As a study aid, you can construct triangles for major points in a chapter, a business letter, a manual, a technical report or a piece of fiction. The reason they work is simple: Since *you* design them, you tend to remember the details of the reading better. The "lasting power" of what you learned from the reading will convince you that these are worth the effort.

Using Writing to Clarify Your Thinking

Often we need **to write** what we think, **to see** what we believe. It's a good reality check. Thoughts you have about a topic prior to reading about it influence how you think. Clarifying thoughts by writing short lists of ideas, feelings or questions can be very helpful. Making "smart remarks" that deal directly with the text, which let you interact with the text on a personal level, will help you clearly see the key points in your reading.

Smart remarks are **comments** or **questions** that let you see, *in writing*, what you really believe or need to know. These remarks are personal comments about what the reading says to you, what it makes you think about or what you feel about it. The idea behind this technique is that your comments, when you go back to look at them or share them aloud with classmates, clearly show what you got out of the text.

This is your chance to see how the "smart remarks" technique works. Read the passage "**Energy, Reactions, and Catalysts,**" and then look at some sample smart remarks that help to clarify thinking about this reading.

How do I know what I think, until I see what I say?

E. M. FORSTER

Energy, Reactions, and Catalysts

Energy is either gained or lost during a chemical change. In some reactions, such as burning, energy is released. In other reactions, energy must be added for a chemical change to occur. If energy is released, the reaction is called exothermic. If energy must be added during a reaction, the reaction is called endothermic.

The burning of magnesium is an exothermic reaction. Though some heat is needed to start the reaction, the heat given off when magnesium bonds with oxygen is more than enough to keep the reaction going.

Heimler and Price. *Focus on Physical Science,* (1981). Columbus,Ohio: Charles E. Merrill.

The following list of comments and questions are examples of what a reader might write to interact with this selected passage.

Smart Remarks

What's a catalyst? Look up or ask.
Adding salt to water should be a chemical change.
*Burning a log in the fireplace releases a lot of energy. The **heat** must be the energy released.*

Exothermic and endothermic—these words remind me of a "thermos" bottle for hot and cold drinks.

Thermometer, thermo-nuclear—are words that must be related.

Energy must EXIT in exothermic reactions. Remember this by the prefix "ex."

How do rechargeable batteries figure into this? Ask about this!

A bomb is major exothermic reaction! Check on this.

*I'm not sure how you can **add energy**?*

These "smart remarks" and questions are personal. There may be more here than you might write. Use these only as examples of one way to interact with the text. You need to see and say what **you** think. Discussing these remarks and questions will help you understand the passage more than reading it over and over. Often when you share your remarks with classmates, you'll see that they can provide answers for you, and you can clear up questions for them. The goal here is for you to **think deeply** about what you read.

ACTIVITY 5: Smart Remarks

Use a passage from your class reading, or use one of the additional readings in the Appendix of this text and make a list of your own smart remarks. Let your remarks really show what you think, what you want to know more about and what related thoughts you have about the topic. Share and discuss these valuable remarks in class.

SUMMARY

This chapter has focused on activities you can do before and after reading that will help you get the most from your efforts. To make meaning when you read, you should do the following:

- preview important words.

- make a written or mental list of those words.

- think about what the words suggest.

- decide what the words mean to you.

Another important way of making meaning is connecting what you already know with what you are reading. Strategies for examining and connecting your thoughts include triangle truths and writing smart remarks. Making connections and seeing applications for what you've read will help you remember and retain information. To make meaning you must interact personally with your reading.

WRITER'S WORKSHOP

Often a passage will contain words, phrases or specific lines that **stand out** from the others. Sometimes these words or phrases are unique, repeated or even highlighted in the text. Like a diamond that sparkles when light hits it, these words or phrases shine in the text as you read it. You should spot these "**diamonds in the rough**" and take note of them. Read the following passage to practice this writing-to-learn technique.

Aging Aircraft

Recently, the general aviation industry has been plagued with a shortage of aircraft. Currently, very few single engine or light twin airplanes are being produced by manufacturers. Research shows, however, that since 1983, the actual number of hours flown in general aviation airplanes has increased from 34 million hours to 36 million hours in 1986. This means more people are flying their older airplanes. This new trend of "hanging on" to older airplanes has brought about the need for more aircraft refurbishing facilities. Only very few professional aviation paint shops exist in the entire Ohio, Kentucky, and Indiana area. The operation of a professional aviation paint shop could fulfill the needs of this entire area.

Philbin and Presley. *Technical Writing*. (1989). Albany, NY: Delmar Publishers, Inc.

Review this passage and be very selective as you do the following:

- Choose several words or phrases that stand out like diamonds in the rough.

- Write the reasons for your selections. Why did these catch your eye?

- Share your words/phrases and reasons with your classmates.

- Decide why these words/phrases are keys to understanding the passage.

A lot of the reading you do has these "**diamonds in the rough**." Finding them helps you understand what the writer thinks is important and what you should focus on. Sometimes a word or phrase shines so brightly that it immediately grabs your attention. These words are worth some thought.

Practice this skill in spotting **key words** and **phrases** in passages from your specific class reading assignments. Choose a short selection, part of a chapter or single piece of writing to apply this to. Make a personal list and compare your selections with your classmates. You may find that your classmates and you will make similar selections. There's a hint there if many readers are picking out similar words and phrases: These words and phrases must be **keys** in the reading.

FINAL CHECK

Answer these questions as a final check of your understanding of this chapter:

1. Preparing to make meaning out of reading can best be done by
   a. first reading the text aloud in a group.
   b. first taking time to make a word find list.
   c. finding related illustrations.
   d. first looking up definitions for all the unknown words.

2. One excellent way to see reading connections and applications is
   a. make guesses about what you think.
   b. write answers to questions at the end of the chapter.
   c. design and share triangle truths.
   d. let others tell you how to connect and apply what you've read.

3. Writing can clarify your thinking when you
   a. write informative notes from the chalkboard.
   b. ask and see what others are thinking.
   c. make long lists of questions from a piece of reading.
   d. honestly write comments to interact with your reading.

Answers: 1. b; 2. c; 3. d

Getting the Big Picture

CHAPTER

4

After completing Chapter Four, you will be able to:

- locate and state the main ideas of a paragraph.

- visually organize information and ideas from a reading into a mind map.

- list and explain other graphic organizers you can use to clarify ideas from a chapter.

- decribe several note taking strategies to use when learning.

Chapter Outline

I. Getting the Main Idea of a Paragraph

II. Making Your Own Mind Map

III. More Examples of Graphic Organizers

IV. About-Point Technique

V. Taking Good Notes

VI. Using Jot Charts

OPENING ACTIVITY

Start to think about the "big picture" of what you have learned so far in the three chapters that you have read. Jot down the main ideas and concepts that you have learned from these three chapters before you begin reading this chapter. Your teacher might want you to share these with the class or with a small group of your classmates.

Getting the Main Idea of a Paragraph

Many readers never see the "big picture" of what is happening in a textbook. A reader should always be attempting to get the "gist" or larger understanding of an entire text or chapter within a text. One way to do this is to begin with getting the "gist" of each paragraph in a passage. A paragraph is a group of sentences that is usually related to a central idea or focal point. This main idea or focal point is the *most important* thing the author wants you to know about the subject. The main idea is usually stated in a topic sentence, which is the one sentence that covers the subject of the entire paragraph. To find the subject, ask *who* or *what* the paragraph is about. The topic sentences are underlined in the next three paragraphs, which are from the same textbook. All of the paragraphs are on the topic of writing resumes for jobs. Notice these topic sentences come at three distinct places in the paragraphs.

Paragraph #1: Topic sentence in middle

Your resume should be detailed enough to give an employer the information needed to judge your qualifications. It should also be brief. *A busy employer wants the important facts in as few words as possible.* In describing your work experience, for example, the sentence, "I was responsible for analyzing the cost sheets from the production department" is too lengthy. It can be condensed into a shorter phrase that provides the same information: "Analyzed production cost sheets."

Paragraph #2: Topic sentence at beginning

In the next section, give a short statement of your career goals. Be specific about the type of job you are seeking. Don't limit yourself to one particular employer, though. (You want to be able to give the resume to many different employers.)

Paragraph #3: Topic sentence at end

If you have limited paid work experience, it is all right to list such paid or unpaid experiences as babysitting, yardwork, newspaper delivery, and so on. You can also mention volunteer work experience such as being a junior volunteer, camp counselor, or campaign worker. *If you think about it, you can probably identify many kinds of work experience that can compensate for having limited paid job experience.*

Bailey, L. *Working Skills For a New Age,* (1990). Albany, NY: Delmar Publishers, pp. 39–40.

A C T I V I T Y 1 : Topic Sentence

Now try these paragraphs to see how you do. Is the main idea or topic sentence the first sentence, in the middle of the paragraph, or at the end of the paragraph?

> The third kind of information is about your education. List all high schools, colleges, technical schools, and so on. Begin with the most recent one. List any diplomas, degrees, licenses, and certificates you earned. Also mention any honors or awards you received. Name any job-related activities in which you participated. For example, Ronald Fisher's performance in an engine troubleshooting contest proves he has diagnostic and mechanical skills.

answer: first sentence

> What happens after you submit the job application form? Do you wait to hear from the employer? Are you supposed to go for an interview or make contact later with the employer? Make sure you find out what to do next. Write the information down on the job-lead card that you are using to keep track of job leads.

answer: last sentence

Bailey, L. *Working Skills For a New Age,* (1990). Albany, NY: Delmar Publishers, pp. 39–40.

Bruce Reiley, © 1981.

Making Your Own Mind Map

Besides finding the main idea in a paragraph, you can identify the main ideas of larger pieces such as chapters or chapter sub-sections. One way to get the big picture of a chapter is to make a visual map of the main aspects of the chapter.

Mapping is a way to:

1. organize information.

2. take notes.

3. show important information.

4. outline.

5. draw a verbal picture of ideas.

6. show how ideas are related.

7. better study and remember.

Figure 4-1

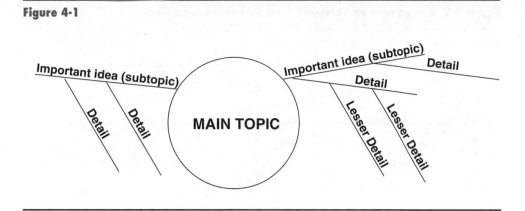

Follow these four basic steps to make a mind map.

1. Print the topic or main idea of the chapter or section in the center of the page. Circle it. (You can also use this procedure for a lecture.)

2. When you read or hear an important idea or fact, (Subtopic) print it on a line that is connected to the circle topic.

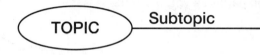

3. Details that explain or describe the important idea are connected to the important idea.

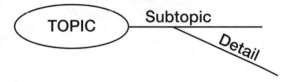

4. Smaller details that explain or describe the detail are connected to the details.

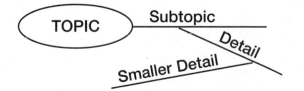

Figure 4-2 **A mind map on "biomes" from an earth science class.**

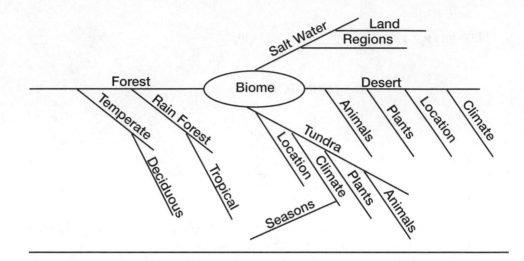

A C T I V I T Y 2 : Graphic Organizer

Following is a section from a business text on controlling monopolies, entitled *Business Principles and Management*. Complete this graphic organizer on a piece of notebook paper as you read the passage.

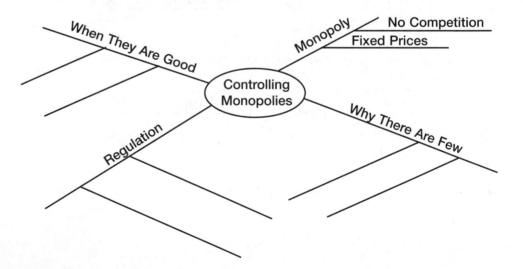

Controlling Monopolies

A monopoly exists when competition is lacking for a product or service, or when producers are in a position to control the supply of goods or services. By controlling the supply of an item, a single producer can set a price that will generate the greatest profit. In business situations where a monopoly exists, prices are generally higher than where competition exists.

In actual practice, however, there are few business monopolies because of the effectiveness of competition. To illustrate, assume a business offers a new product that no other business has. The product suddenly becomes quite popular. Other companies now enter the market to help meet the demand. A temporary monopoly will exist until those competitors can produce and sell similar products. Usually, through competitive pricing, the more efficient companies will attract the greatest number of purchasers while the less efficient may struggle for survival or go out of business. Even if some competitors fail, however, monopolies can be preferred over competition. These situations usually involve providing public services which have a fairly stable demand and which are costly to create like public utilities. A natural gas company, for example, must build hundreds of miles of pipeline along streets and roads in order to deliver gas to homes and industries to fuel furnaces, stoves, and equipment. If two or three gas companies incurred these same costs to sell gas to a relatively fixed number of customers, the price of gas would be higher than if only one company existed. Also, installing and maintaining so many pipelines would create nuisance problems along crowded streets and highways. In these types of situations, therefore, a monopoly is more desirable than competition. When the government grants a monopoly to a company, it usually controls the prices that can be charged and influences other company policies.

Until recently, the federal government had approved of closely regulated monopolies, such as the postal system, utility companies, railroads, and communication firms. However, the trend has shifted from approving of monopolies to weakening or eliminating them in order to encourage competition. No longer, for example, are passenger fares on commercial airlines heavily regulated. As a result, fares have dropped. Even telephone services at competitive prices now freely compete with American Telephone & Telegraph (AT&T).

Reading Maketh A Full Man 99

NATHANIEL BACON

Evard, K. and Burrow, J. *Business Principles & Management, 9th ed.,* (1990). Cincinnati: South-Western Publishing Co., pp. 64–65.

More Examples of Graphic Organizers

Remember, there is no "right" or "wrong" way to record and display information using a graphic organizer format. These graphic displays do sometimes offer a better alternative to learning than the traditional outline because you can record more depth of understanding and more clearly show the relationships among facts and concepts.

Following are examples of graphic organizers from two different sources:

A. Interviewing from a text in business. (Figure 4-3)

B. Problems with the centering adjustment of a SONY camera based on information from a service manual. (Figure 4-4)

Figure 4-3

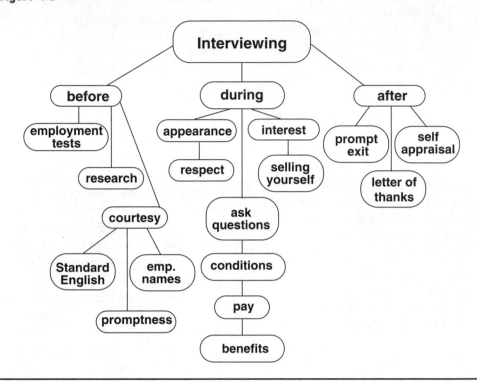

Figure 4-4

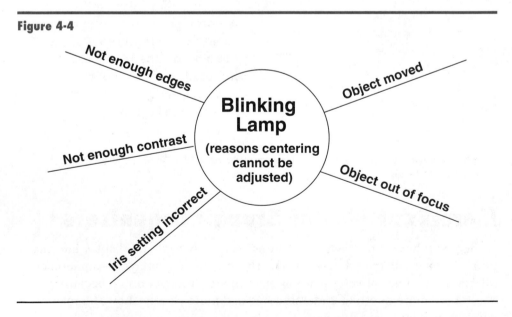

About-Point Technique

Many times, after assigning a chapter to be read, a teacher will ask students, "What is this material saying?" The teacher is *not* asking for details, but for overall meaning. This type of reading task requires a different mindset on the part of the student: a THINK BIG mindset. The following selection is concerned with "expectation." When you finish previewing and reading, complete the "ABOUT-POINT" activities then ask yourself, "What was this selection about?" You should be able to formulate a clear statement of understanding.

A C T I V I T Y   3 :   What is the Point?

Net sales volume, often referred to as **sales volume** or **operating income**, is the total amount of dollars received from the sale of merchandise, less customer returns and allowances, sales taxes, and the retailer's excise taxes collected directly from customers (e.g., gasoline) for a specific period of time. Net sales volume represents what the customer is willing to pay.

This paragraph is ABOUT:

and the POINT is:

The financial guide to the success of any retail operation is the **income statement**, also referred to as the **profit and loss statement (P&L)** or **operating statement**. The income statement serves two purposes:

1. It provides financial data for income tax reporting and other required legal reports.

2. It reports the recent results of merchandising and operating decisions.

Usually prepared monthly, with quarterly and annual recaps, the income statement reveals net sales volume, cost of goods sold, gross margin of profit, all related operating expenses (fixed and variable), net operating profit or loss, and net profit or loss after other income, other expenses, and income taxes.

These paragraphs are ABOUT:

and the POINT is:

Paidar, M. *Merchandising Mathematics,* (1994). Albany, NY: Delmar Publishers, pp. 48–49.

Taking Good Notes

All the techniques we have discussed in this chapter up to this point are about how to recognize key ideas from reading or how to organize them into useful visual diagrams. Another important skill is taking quality notes from which to study. Good notes always focus on the big picture, but allow you to keep tabs on the details related to the main idea. As a result, good notes are easy to study from.

Two-Column Notes

One of the most effective ways of taking notes is to divide your paper into two columns by drawing a line down the page one third of the way from the left side of the page.

Two-column notes as described in Figure 4-5 are very effective because the left column gives you "intellectual space" to think about the big points made in the text or the lecture. Then smaller points can be filled in on the right side as the reading or lecture progresses.

Figure 4-5 Two-column notes

Culture and Identity	
1. Subculture	1. Differing groups 2. Have certain characteristics 3. Different characteristics than those of larger, common culture
2. Ethnic Groups	1. Values 2. Customs 3. Common history and ancestry 4. Experiences are unique 5. Can be a race, religion, nationality, or language
3. Heritage	1. What is handed down from generation to generation 2. Inheritance 3. Ethnicity 4. Learned through subculture

Studying With Two-Column Notes

Two-column notes can also help you study. Fold over two-thirds of the page to cover the details and quiz yourself about the details that relate to the main ideas. (See Figure 4-6.) If you can't remember all of the details, you can peek under the folded part, and then try again.

Two-column Notes from Lectures

If a teacher lectures, but does not always clearly state the main ideas or objectives, simply take all your notes on the right side of the paper, leaving the left one-third blank. If you go back over your notes within the first 8-24 hours, you will be able to figure out the main ideas of the lecture and label the left side of your sheet. Then use the left side for study purposes. Many successful students highlight or underline key words from the lecture when they go over it in review. This makes a second or third reading even easier to do.

Figure 4-6 Studying from two-column notes

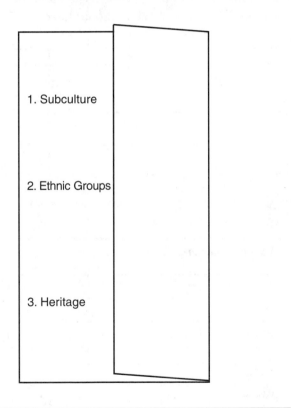

1. Subculture

2. Ethnic Groups

3. Heritage

ACTIVITY 4 : Using Two-column Notes

Now use two-column note taking in one of your classes to improve your ability to take notes. Ask your teacher to allow you to share your notes with another member of the class who has taken notes on the same material. Compare notes to see if you wrote the same things and share ways that you can improve the notes.

Using Jot Charts

Another note-taking technique similar to two-column note taking is the use of jot charts. These also relate main ideas to important details or concepts. Jot charts are especially useful for comparing and contrasting various things. In a jot chart you write descriptions of the concepts you are studying across the top of the chart. These descriptions can sometimes be major concepts covered in the chapter. Sometimes, chapter headings or sub-headings can serve as the "features" across the top of the chart. The main topics you are studying are placed down the side of the chart. It should look like this:

Topics	Descriptions				

The following illustration compares two dinosaur species.

Figure 4-7 Jot Chart of Dinosaurs

Dinosaur Species	Description	Method of Birth	Embryo Development at Hatching	Parental Feeding of Newborn	Parental Protection of Newborn
Orodromeus makelai	• Walked on 2 legs • 8 feet high • Embryos 8"-9"	• Hatched from eggs	• Bones developed • Able to walk	• Probably did *not* bring food to nest	• Probably did *not* protect
Maiasaura peeblesorum (duck bills)	• Walked on 2 legs • 30 feet high • Embryos 1"	• Hatched from eggs	• Bones *not* developed • Unable to walk	• Probably did bring food to nest	• Probably did protect

Richardson, J. and Morgan, R. *Reading to Learn in the Content Areas, 2nd ed.,* (1994). Belmont, CA: Wadsworth, p. 218.

Chapter 4 Getting the Big Picture

ACTIVITY 5 : Practice with a Jot Chart

Copy the following jot chart onto your own paper. Then read the following segment on pages 59–61 from *Computers and Information Processing: Concepts and Applications* and record in the chart important details relating to three ways of putting data into computers.

Type of Input Device	Description	How Used	Kinds of Raw Data Stored
Scanning Device			
Keyboard			
Source Document			

Input-Putting Data into the Computer

Chapter Objectives
After reading this chapter, you should be able to...
- Identify sources of raw data and explain how input devices are used to put data into the computer.
- Identify and explain the usage of several of the more common input devices.
- Identify several special purpose input devices.
- Define terminals and describe the difference between local and remote terminals.

Introduction
Input devices are used to enter software instruction (programs) and data into a computer's memory. After a computer program has been entered into the computer's memory and it begins to execute, it can direct the processor to read data from any input device which is connected to the computer. The specific input device and the manner in which the data is entered into the computer's memory is controlled entirely by instructions provided by a computer program. In this chapter, you will learn more about data and the types of input devices used to enter it into the computer.

What is Data?
You learned in Chapter 2 that data consists of facts in the form of num-

(Continued on the following page)

bers, alphabetic characters, special symbols, or words. Computers are used as tools to process or manipulate data into information which humans can use to obtain new knowledge. The data which is fed into a computer for processing is commonly referred to as raw data or original data. This is because this type of data is of no value by itself; however, when combined with other data, it creates useful information. Raw data that is input into a computer system comes from two sources: it is input directly into the computer as it is originated, or it is first recorded on a form and then fed into the computer at a later time.

Raw data that is input directly into the computer at the time it originates is often entered via the keyboard, read by a scanning device, or input by sound (i.e. human voice, telephone). For example, many law enforcement officers have keyboards and display screens in their cars for immediate access to information stored in a mainframe computer. When they need to check a car to see if it has been stolen, the license number can be keyed directly into the computer. Once the number has been keyed, the mainframe computer searches its files of vehicle license plate numbers until it finds a matching number. It then displays information regarding the known status of the vehicle in question on the officer's display screen.

Another example of raw data that is input directly into the computer is a sale of merchandise. Many retail stores use devices which can scan a sales tag and input the data regarding the type of merchandise sold, sales price, etc., directly into a computer at the time of the sale. The use of a push button telephone is another common example of directly inputting raw data into the computer. Many telephone carriers permit their customers to make long distance calls from anywhere in the country by keying-in their authorization codes using the telephone's push buttons. Each press of a key creates a pitched tone which the computer recognizes as the customer's authorization code. It then checks its file to make sure the code is valid before it permits the caller to place the call.

A handwritten form containing raw data that is to be input into a computer is called a source document. It is called a source document because it is prepared by individuals who originate, or create, the raw data it contains. For example, many large companies have individuals who are employees in what is called a payroll department. It is their job to make sure that each of the company's employees receives his/her payroll check accurately and on time. They prepare a payroll input from containing the employee name and number, hours worked, overtime hours, etc., for each employee to be paid each pay period. The information contained on this form is keyed into the computer. The computer then prepares the necessary company payroll reports and employee paychecks for the payroll period. Source documents come from many different sources for many different computer applications.

Types of Data Input Devices

Input devices come in many sizes and shapes, operate at different speeds, and have different capacities and capabilities. Many computers have more than one input device attached to facilitate various types of processing which must be performed. In many instances, the task that must be accomplished determines which input device is best to use. In other instances, input devices have been specially designed and developed to facilitate specific types of input and processing. In this section, we will discuss several of the more commonly used input devices.

Keyboard

The computer keyboard is the most popular and common way of inputting data into the computer. The keyboard of a computer is similar to that of a typewriter. When a key is pressed, the corresponding alphabetic, numeric, or special symbol is converted into a code and electronically sent to the computer's memory. Once the desired character is stored in memory, it becomes accessible for processing by the stored program.

Clark, J., Allen, W., and Klooster, D. *Computers and Information Processing: Concepts and Applications, 2nd ed.*, (1990). Cincinnati, Ohio: South-Western Publishing Co.

SUMMARY

Students often have difficulty seeing the "big picture"—gaining larger under-standing of a reading selection. Strategies for getting the big picture include:

- mind mapping

- graphic organizers

- About-Point techniques

- jot charts

- two-column note taking

These techniques aid in comprehension in reading. All of these strategies are an attempt by the reader to clarify thinking while reading. Constantly clari-fying your thinking while reading will result in more comprehension of the reading materials.

WRITER'S WORKSHOP 1

Here are some terms discussed in this chapter:

About-Point	two-column notes
jot chart	gist
paragraph	graphic organizer
mind map	big picture
facts	concepts
relationships	

Take these terms and on your own sheet of paper make a graphic organiz-er depicting the relationship of the terms as you have learned them. Try it this way:

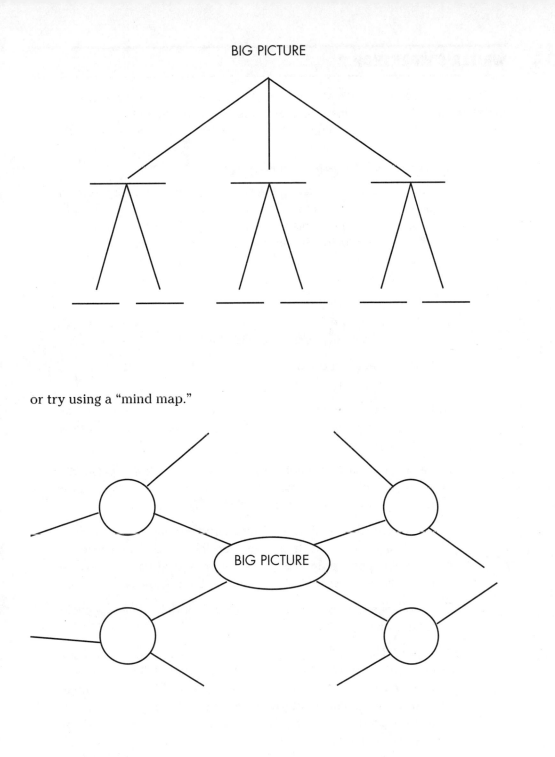

BIG PICTURE

or try using a "mind map."

BIG PICTURE

Following is a Sears Service Manual on Floor Covering describing ways an installer should act when visiting a customer's home. On a sheet of paper turn these points into two-column notes using the method we learned in this chapter.

II. BEHAVIOR IN THE CUSTOMER'S HOME

1. Installer personnel entering the customer's home are representing Sears, and as such must conduct themselves accordingly. They must demonstrate the highest degree of professional behavior at all times. In addition their personal grooming must reflect this affiliation with Sears—clothing clean and well kept, hair well kept, beards neatly trimmed or fully shaven (no 2 day growth), etc.

2. When initially arriving at the customer's home present to the customer the Sears authorized installer card.

3. Installer personnel are not to smoke or eat in the customer's home.

4. Installer personnel are not to use the customer's phone for personal use. With permission, the customer's phone may be used for business purposes.

5. Installer personnel are not to use any of the customer's personal property. With the customer's permission, they may bring a radio to the job. In this instance, the volume must be kept low.

6. No personnel shall discuss with the customer anything regarding the quality, style, or type of Home Fashions product purchased. Rather, be positive and complimentary of the customer's choice— it reflects her personal taste which should be respected.

7. Personnel must take care not to track dirt or debris into the customer's home.

8. The installer is in the home as a result of a successfully sold Sears lead. This lead was the property of Sears and all further leads which result from it are likewise the property of Sears. If any new leads result while the installer is on the job (for any business Sears engages in) said leads must be given to the DCSU, or store sales associate/decorator.

Sears, Roebuck & Co. *Home Fashions Instruction Manual.* Chicago, IL: Sears, Roebuck & Co. Used with permission.

FINAL CHECK

Answer these questions a a final check on your understanding of this chapter:

1. The most important thing that the author wants you to know about the subject is:
   a. to recall the title.
   b. to learn the main idea of the passage.
   c. to recall all the facts without mistake.
   d. to learn all the big vocabulary words in a chapter.

2. It is important as you read to always:
   a. clarify you thinking.
   b. only look at the pictures.
   c. look up all the big words in a dictionary.
   d. practice reading the chapter aloud.

3. Graphic organizers are a way for students to:
   a. look up difficult words in a dictionary.
   b. organize the textbook in outline form.
   c. make a mind map showing relationships of concepts in a chapter.
   d. impress their friends.

Answers: 1. b; 2. a; 3. c

Reading and Writing Narratives

CHAPTER 5

CHAPTER OBJECTIVES

This chapter will show you helpful ways to read and write narratives. The skills you practice with narratives can be applied to all other types of reading and writing. After completing Chapter Five, you will be able to:

● describe what a narrative is.

● determine what is different about narratives.

● make better predictions about outcomes of narratives.

● use clues to read narratives.

● learn ways to write your own narrative.

Chapter Outline

I. Why Read and Study Narratives?

II. What is a Narrative?

III. What is Different About Narratives?

IV. Making Predictions to Understand Narratives

V. Writing Narratives

VI. Tips on Writing Your Own Narrative

OPENING ACTIVITY

After you've read this paragraph, write five questions about this story. Begin each with one of the following words: **who**, **what**, **when**, **where** and **why**. Your questions, when answered, should give you more specific information about what you've read or make the story more clear.

Title _____

At exactly 6:37 p.m., the 6 o'clock train on the New Haven Line pulled into a foggy Columbus Avenue Park Station. On this October evening, the few people waiting on the platform did not notice Dan Hannon as he quickly stepped down from the train. Gripping a battered, gray-tweed satchel with both hands he made his way from the platform through the deserted station. Also going unnoticed, was Dan's stream-lined suit. After walking through the station without incident, Dan stopped in front of a huge oak door that had been scarred by the briefcases of rushing commuters late for their trains. With a shudder, as the awful memory flashed in his brain, he pushed open the door leading to Columbus Avenue Park.

After writing your questions, decide on a **title** for this narrative. Give a reason to support your chosen title. Share these titles with your classmates. Can you see how their titles might also fit the story?

Why Read and Study Narratives?

A reader makes a story come alive with imagination, feeling and thoughts. As you read a well written narrative you become captivated by the "story." You start with the opening paragraph and follow it naturally to its conclusion. A lot of the reading, listening and writing that you do in school requires that you **follow a series** of events **in sequence**, as well. Think about some of the activities you do that require sequencing skills in reading, listening and writing:

- a story in literature
- a word problem in math
- an account of an event in history
- an experiment in science
- a procedure in technology
- a proposal in business
- rules for a game in physical education
- a set of instructions for a project

Reading, writing and listening to narratives gives you experience in these practical skills that help you see a logical sequence of events. These skills help you to **follow** the story, to **understand** what's happening and why, and to **remember** important points in it.

With practice it will be easier to see an order or pattern develop in a story. This ability to see, follow and think in an orderly way transfers to what you do in any occupation you choose. It helps you read and write better. Look at a few of the tasks you might face on the job and consider the skills you would need:

- to follow a manual.
- to give instructions or directions.
- to place a detailed order.
- to outline steps for action.

> *The unread story is not a story; it is little black marks on wood pulp. The reader, reading it, makes it live: a live thing, a story.*
>
> URSULA K. LE GUIN

- to write a business letter.

- to give a report.

- to create or modify a plan.

In all of these cases, an organized and ordered sequence is necessary to complete the task. Narratives are an interesting, engaging and enjoyable way to naturally acquire these essential skills. You can practice with narratives in three ways:

1. Look at the parts of a narrative.

2. Focus on specific clue words for understanding.

3. Use hints to write your own narrative.

You can transfer what you learn about reading and writing narratives to every other language activity you may be asked to do.

This activity will use a sample of writing that often is required for getting a job. Review the sentences from a letter of recommendation that an employer wrote for one of his employees. Put them in a *logical order* or sequence that makes sense.

To:	Ms. Ellen Whitley, Personnel Director
From:	Thomas Horton, Dept. Head of Hersch Labs, Inc.
Re:	Letter of Recommendation for Lauren Johnson

Dear Ms. Whitley:

A. She is dedicated to maintaining high standards of performance on the job.

B. Lauren is cooperative, self-motivated and eager to solve problems.

C. Lauren is a competent technician who has excellent abilities in her field, and she possesses an extensive knowledge of chemistry.

D. Please contact me if I can be of further assistance to you in your decision to hire Ms. Johnson.

E. She has received excellent yearly evaluation ratings for each of the three years she has worked for us.

F. Lauren Johnson has demonstrated her ability to work well on a team, and she would be a valuable addition to any staff fortunate enough to be able to benefit from her expertise.

G. I am writing to recommend Lauren Johnson as head lab technician for your company.

H. While Hersch Labs, Inc. regrets that it is necessary for Lauren to relocate, we are confident in recommending her highly and without hesitation.

I. I have supervised her work as an assistant lab chemist in our pharmaceutical department for three years.

A logical sequence or pattern that makes sense can be followed more easily by a reader. It's possible that you may have put the sentences from the recommendation in a slightly different order than one of your class-mates. That's fine; there may be more than one good way to order these sentences. It's important to practice ordering and to recognize a logical pattern. Narratives often follow a chronological or time order sequence, but you'll notice a sequence or logical pattern in everything you read.

For example, in the letter of recommendation, can you see why the sentence labeled "A" would not be suitable for an opening sentence? It would not be logical to put this sentence in this position in the letter. Look at the sentence again:

A. She is dedicated to maintaining high standards of performance on the job.

If this sentence appeared first in the recommendation, the employer receiving this wouldn't know one critical piece of information: what "job" did this person perform with high standards? It's also not a good idea to refer to the person as "she" without first giving her full name in the body of the letter. This sentence would be best placed elsewhere in the recommendation letter.

What is a Narrative?

A good narrative gets a reader to reflect upon it based on personal experiences and feelings. When you reflect on the story, you become involved in it. You ask questions, sometimes unconsciously, that cause you to read on for the answers. Good narratives keep listeners and readers interested to do this. A good story makes a reader want to know more. A good reader uses imagination to think about the story beyond the words that are printed.

Often, the beginning paragraph or paragraphs of a narrative answer many questions for the reader. Pay attention to these. You can often tell what the story will be about, who the main character is, what the problem is, and where and when the action takes place. Sometimes understanding why the action is occurring or why a character acts in a certain way comes a bit later, after you reflect and digest the story. Good readers **question**, **reflect** and **digest** during and after reading a story. If the first few paragraphs don't give you a clear view, the solution is easy: **keep alert** . . . and **keep reading**.

Reflecting on a One-Minute Short Story

Read the sample sentence below and determine if it is a story.

> Bob went to the beach to see the ship passing by the island.

Does it have a character, a setting, some action and some meaning? If so, then it does qualify as a one-minute (maybe less to write) short story. So, what's missing? What will make this story more interesting for the reader? Read the next sentences in the boxes to see how some **simple additions** can make this a more interesting story.

1. Add a *what* and a *why*:

> Bob ran to the beach, but the ship was too distant to hear his cry for help.

2. Add a *what* and a *who*:

> He turned in the direction of his signal fire and saw that Judy had let it go out.

Reading a book is like re-writing it for yourself. . . . You bring to a novel, anything you read, all your experience of the world. You bring your history and you read it in your own terms.

ANGELA CARTER

3. Add a *why*:

> Judy strolled out of the jungle carrying an armful of bananas and said, "Hey, Bob, look what I found!"

You can create a better story by slightly adjusting or adding to the following elements that make up any story:

Character(s)   **Dialogue**   **Plot**   **Setting**

Meaning   **Conflict**

With just these three sentences, you can see a way to create *a full* story. One addition many readers like is dialogue. It lets them hear the characters speak on the page and in their minds. You can see how adding a few sentences to the one-minute story makes it more involved and more interesting.

A C T I V I T Y   2 :   Writing A One-Minute Story

Write your own one-minute story. Start with the basic necessities. Use something like our sample starter sentence:

who	where	why	what
Bob	went to the beach	to see the ship passing	by the island.

Add words, phrases or sentences like in the sample to build your own one-minute short story. Keep them short and focused. Share these with your group or others.

What is Different About Narratives?

A seer is someone who can see ahead, who uses what's known to predict what will happen. Guesses rely on what's known to help make the predictions of the future more accurate. When you are reading for information or reading to find out what will come next, there are ways to increase your efficiency.

Many of the same strategies you use to understand information written in a textbook apply in a narrative:

- **previewing** specific sections
- **looking** at the pictures or graphics
- **skimming** the story first
- **focusing** on the opening or ending
- **hearing** the story read aloud

- **listing** specific words that need defining

- **reading** the narrative twice

So, what's different? Narrative writing naturally invites you to follow along and get involved in the story. Some informative texts don't require this type of personal involvement. In other words, in a textbook, a reader sometimes reads for specific information or with a specific reason. This information, for instance, can be in the form of a statistic or definition that the reader needs to know to answer a question.

One example would be when you look up a definition of a word in a dictionary. You aren't reading a story; you just want information, a written meaning, about a word. The search for this information is focused and leads to a definite end.

In another example, imagine that you are reading a manual on installing a ceiling fan. You have a definite purpose in reading for information. You need to know what color wire to connect to make the fan turn, so you search the manual for the section and line where this information is listed. You read it in a very specific way.

So, reading a story *is* different. In narratives, the **story** is the most important aspect. You are interested in knowing **what happens** overall. First, you read the story to get a sense of the entire piece. Then, you might go back to read parts again to review specifics. Although reading stories appears slightly different in this way, you use many of the same skills you would use with any type of reading.

Showing vs. Telling

Narratives, like anything you read, have something to tell. The difference in a story or narrative is that *the story, not the writer* specifically, speaks to the reader. For example, when you write a note to a friend or an answer to a question on a test, the reader of these pieces recognizes that **you** are speaking through the words you've written.

In narratives, though, the writer is not always so clearly defined. A story **shows** more than it **tells** directly. The reader finds the meaning in the story itself or in a character's actions. For example, assume a writer wants to show a character who is "dedicated." A line from a narrative might read something like this:

Allison spent hour after hour sitting on the park bench carefully sketching each detail of the faces she saw in the crowd.

This one line **shows** Allison, who is hardworking or "dedicated." This **meaning** based on Allison's actions must be supplied by the reader though; the writer doesn't tell us this directly but only shows or describes the way Allison sketches. The reader must come up with answers to the following questions to get the full meaning of this behavior:

1. Does Allison love to sketch people?

2. Does she take her art seriously?

3. How careful is she about details?

The reader determines more meaning than the writer tells directly. Based on this line, what are some other ideas you have about Allison?

A C T I V I T Y 3 : Showing vs. Telling

Choose a word from the following list and using any character of your choice write a sentence that shows instead of tells. Don't use the word you selected in your sentence. Share the sentences, not your word, with your classmates to see if they can determine what you are trying to show.

exhaustion	boredom	worry	confusion
anger	hysteria	arrogance	defiance
obedient	peaceful	sadness	surprised
content	friendly	greed	togetherness
excited	thankful	courtesy	inconsiderate
strict	wild	shy	thoughtful

Make a different class list of words and practice this activity. You can use words related to your subject or lesson.

Making Predictions to Understand Narratives

One of the best strategies to help you understand and involve you in a narrative is to make predictions or speculate on what will happen. You can afford to guess early in your reading. The story will unfold more clearly for you if you practice this technique. You can use a lot of clues that the story provides. You can get ideas in a lot of ways:

- based on selected words (practiced earlier)
- by the title
- by the setting description
- by the dialogue between the characters
- by the actions of the characters

These can all help you to tune into a story. Stop every few paragraphs and predict or ask questions. Above all, relax! These ideas are yours so that you can interact with the narrative as it unfolds.

To get a clear picture of what you're reading, it's useful to ask questions and make predictions based on the text. Some readers do this mentally as they're reading, but to learn the technique, at least at first, it would be a good idea to jot down these questions and predictions in a notebook. You can refer to these after you've completed your reading to be sure that you can clarify anything that is still not making sense to you. On page 76 is an example of how this technique looks using the paragraph you've already seen in the Opening Activity. Notice the predictions and questions which you also may have thought about when you read the story.

A C T I V I T Y 4 : Making Predictions

Try this technique with the opening paragraph of the narrative that follows.

The Collection

As he had done for the last four nights, Tony Scavo, a small, nervous man, entered the clearing by the same small worn path. Tony walked directly to the far end of the open space and sat on the trunk of a fallen tree. He searched the clearing with his eyes. He had to squint to see through plumes of mist rising toward the tops of the giant pines surrounding him. Tony cupped his right ear with his hand. He listened intently to the faint sounds coming from the forest around him. He mentally noted that this would be absolutely the last stop tonight. He also noted, that up to this point, it had been a very unproductive evening. He desperately needed to return with some proof. He leaned forward with clasped hands and both elbows resting on his knees to steady his gaze on the clearing. That's when, through the mist, he saw it. And it was perfect!

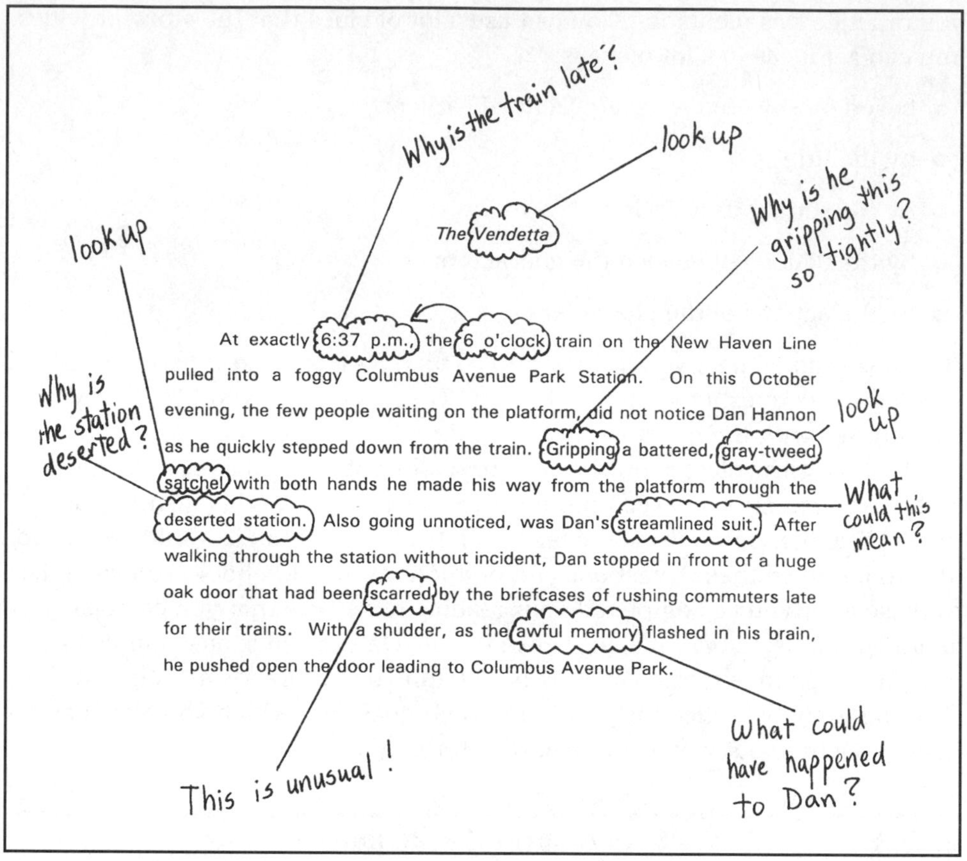

The Vendetta

At exactly 6:37 p.m., the 6 o'clock train on the New Haven Line pulled into a foggy Columbus Avenue Park Station. On this October evening, the few people waiting on the platform, did not notice Dan Hannon as he quickly stepped down from the train. Gripping a battered, gray-tweed satchel with both hands he made his way from the platform through the deserted station. Also going unnoticed, was Dan's streamlined suit. After walking through the station without incident, Dan stopped in front of a huge oak door that had been scarred by the briefcases of rushing commuters late for their trains. With a shudder, as the awful memory flashed in his brain, he pushed open the door leading to Columbus Avenue Park.

Why is the train late?
look up
Why is he gripping this so tightly?
look up
Why is the station deserted?
look up
What could this mean?
This is unusual!
What could have happened to Dan?

As you review your questions and predictions for "The Collection," choose a few essential ones to share with your classmates. Give your reasons for your selections. Compare these to see similarities and differences in your reading of the paragraph.

Writing Narratives

One of the best ways to improve your reading skills with narratives or any other type of reading material is to practice producing a sample yourself. You've told a lot of stories, listened to narrative tales, watched them in films and read them in literature books, yet the chance to write a narrative of your own is probably more rare for you. Trying to write your own narrative gives you greater appreciation for stories that you read.

Before you can **share and show** a story, you need to have an idea. Begin by brainstorming story ideas, and let them flow through your mind. Don't leave out any ideas. When a particular idea that you like strikes you, expand on it and make as many connections as you can think of. Keep alert to what people say and do during daily life for possible story material and characters. Sometimes an A to Z list helps generate ideas.

A C T I V I T Y 5 : Ideas from A to Z

You can make an A to Z list to help you get ideas for a story. On a piece of paper, write the first letters of the alphabet down the left side. Take a few minutes and go through the alphabet, skipping letters if you have no words to write for the letter, and write words or phrases that begin with each of the letters. This quick list can be helpful to get ideas. See our sample below:

A Angels, Around the Block, Always Crying, Alive

B Baby, Baseball Game, Bikes, Bluefish,

C Cars, Crazy Clothes, Cool Stuff, Casey

D Deer, Drums, Disaster, Death, Ducks

E Eating Worms, Eggs, Elevators, Eleven

Any one of these words or phrases can be expanded into an idea for a story. Use these only as a starting point. This is only one way to get ideas. Reading, talking, remembering, connecting, and observing are also possible ways for you to think of a story idea.

Tips on Writing Your Own Narrative

Why should we write our own stories? Well, like almost any activity we can better understand it if we try it ourselves. By trying to write a narrative, we better understand how to read, interpret and enjoy stories written by other writers.

Storytelling as a form of entertainment or way to transfer knowledge and traditions. While we all need to satisfy basic living necessities, we also need more in life to be satisfied and happy. We tell stories from the earliest stages

> *When I get a little money, I buy books; and if any is left, I buy food and clothes.*
>
> DESIDERIUS ERASMUS

of our oral and written communication. And since it is such an old habit and necessary skill, the more we practice it the better storytellers and writers we become.

Find a book of short stories. You can find many of these in your school library. You won't have to read all of the stories, but you should use them to help guide you for the *format* of writing your own. Use any story as a model for setting up your own.

1. Read ***opening lines*** and ***first paragraphs*** of stories in your text to see effective ways to begin yours. Spend time on writing your opening.

2. Look at dialogue and characters' actions and let these tell your story! Read the following samples. See how the second version *shows* the reader rather than *tells*.

   A. Mark was very tired. He had really had an awful day.

   B. Mark sighed and fell heavily onto the couch and looked at Liz. "What is it?" she asked.
   "I've had it," he said. "You can't imagine what those customers did to me today!"

3. Avoid using too many showy verbs of saying. It distracts the reader if your characters whine, exclaim, scream, bark, snort, whimper or bellow too much. Use *said* most of the time. Use *Willy said* instead of, *said Willy* (an old style). At times when it is clear who is speaking, you don't need a verb of saying. Switch paragraphs whenever a new speaker speaks so your reader can follow the conversation easily. Something like this example is easy to follow:

   "Yes, what can I do for you?" Willy asked.
   "I'd like an application for work."
   "Well, we're really not hiring anyone now. But if you want to check back in a few months, maybe we'll need someone."
   "Oh, but I think you *need* to hire me. . . now!"
   "Yeah, and why is that?"
   The old woman looked at him steadily and said, "Because I can make your business worth a million dollars."

4. Make dialogue realistic and necessary. It should **"sound right"** for the character. It should move the story along and be important for the reader.

5. Since each change in speaker requires that you start a new paragraph, check the patterns of punctuation. See the sample below:

   "Wait here, " Louis said. "I'll just be a minute. Why don't you make yourself comfortable?"
   "Okay," Maria said. "You just hurry back. You hear?"
   "When I get back," Louis said, looking directly into her eyes, "we'll discuss what to do with our money."
   Maria said, "What d'ya mean, our. . .?" but Louis was gone before she could finish her question.

S U M M A R Y

Reading and writing narratives can help you develop skills important to reading many other types of materials, specifically:

- following the sequence of a narrative.

- understanding what's happening and why.

- remembering important points.

Good readers question, reflect and digest as they read. They use many of the same skills with narratives used to understand information in a textbook, including:

- previewing.

- looking at pictures or graphics.

- skimming.

- focusing on the beginning or ending.

- hearing the story.

- listing words to be defined.

- reading the narrative twice.

- predicting.

Narratives are different from informative texts, though, in that they invite the reader to become involved in the story and may show more information indirectly than they tell directly.

Writer's Workshop

Use your story from Activity 2—Writing a One-Minute Story or your idea from Activity 5—Ideas from A to Z to write your own narrative. You may have to go back to review these activities to create a story.

1. Decide early on why you are telling your story. For example, a story might show how having inconsiderate neighbors can affect you or how a friend can help you in a time of need.

2. Select a **format** and a **voice**. In other words, decide who will tell the story. You can use the first person voice "**I**" or you can use the third person voice. "**The girl**" watched, "**Leslie**" decided and "**she**" walked away, are examples of third person voice. You can tell the story in the past tense or in the present tense.

3. Decide on real time for the plot to occur. A few minutes in a doctor's office or an afternoon at the beach can be workable time frames.

4. Visualize the length of the story. Consider the number of events in the plot and the length of the conversations to make this **workable and reasonable**. As you create the story, build it by adding parts. Start with a character, an action and add to this as you write. You should keep your narrative short and on target.

5. Consider using a limited number of characters. Consider their real purpose and necessity in the story. A grandfather and his grandson sitting on the porch talking about a problem or an employer firing a worker are good examples.

6. Make your characters different from each other to **heighten the sense of conflict**. The conflict is the main tension or problem in the story. It can be as simple as a physical struggle to climb a mountain or as complex as making a decision that will affect a character's life. Make the conflict strong.

7. Create dialogue for your characters. Make sure the dialogue moves the story along or gives the reader insight into the characters. For example consider the character of a young child who screams at her mother, "You can't make me eat lima beans!" Your reader can tell a lot about that child through just that short piece of dialogue. Let the child's words **reveal** his personality and **create** his description.

8. Read the story and dialogue aloud to hear how the story flows. Try out specific pieces of the story on listeners or readers. Encourage them to ask you questions. Ask them what they don't understand. They can fill in questions that start like this:

> I don't understand why. . . ?
>
> I don't understand how. . . ?
>
> I don't understand what. . . ?
>
> I don't understand when. . . ?

If readers can follow your story and are interested to know more, you've been successful. Share your finished stories with your classmates.

FINAL CHECK

Answer these questions as a final check on your understanding of this chapter.

1. By looking at the words a writer uses in narratives, a reader can:
   a. learn to pronounce all the words.
   b. learn how a writer feels about the events in a story.
   c. make certain that at the end of a story, comprehension questions can be answered.
   d. look up the biggest words in a dictionary.

2. A narrative is:
   a. the contextual pre-figuration of a story.
   b. the gestures and symbols of a story.
   c. writing that tells a story.
   d. writing that teaches basic concepts.

3. Writing your own narrative can:
   a. be one way to read longer texts.
   b. help you become a better storyteller.
   c. be a way to get published.
   d. improve all forms of writing.

Answers: 1. b; 2. c; 3. d

Strategies for Effective Thinking

CHAPTER 6

CHAPTER OBJECTIVES

After completing Chapter Six, you will be able to:

- define critical thinking and explain why critical thinking is important.
- describe thinking at three different levels.
- practice three level thinking.
- describe how to practice thinking at six different levels.

Chapter Outline

OPENING ACTIVITY

Take the time to preview this chapter. After you have done so, scan the list of words below. Divide a sheet of paper into three columns. Label the first column, "Words I Know Well." Label the second column, "Words I Am Not Sure About." Label the third column, "Words I Don't Know." Take the words listed here, and put each one in one of the columns you have made. Do this before you start reading the chapter. Prepare yourself to locate and pay special attention to what they mean in the chapter.

thinking
critical thinking
literal level thinking
inferential thinking
application level thinking
cubing
analyzing

Thinking is...

like the ability to move or

perform as an athlete

or a dancer...

without training, the body

does not move with style and grace...

The same is true for the mind.

without instruction

and practice,

it does not function very well...

we must prepare and train for

intellectual performance.

with rehearsal, practice, and coaching.

Author Unknown

Why Critical Thinking is Important

Imagine yourself in the following situation. You are the supervisor of a particular assembly operation at an automobile manufacturing plant. Working under your supervision are two employees whom you have personally trained, and whose work monitoring robots has been consistently excellent. The machines they monitor place welds at various locations on the autos as they come past on the assembly line. Much of what they do involves watching the welding process and then inspecting the welds after they are made. Both of your workers were trained as welders in high school. They are both always on time and do whatever you tell them without complaint, and they perform to the best of their ability.

When a problem occurs with the strength of the welds over a period of time, you are told by your supervisor to find out where the problem is. However, when you present the problem to your two workers, their responses are different. When told that the strength of some of the welds has been questioned, and that they need to help you trouble-shoot the problem, Worker A says that both he and Worker B have done a flawless job of monitoring the robots and the materials that they have used. He knows that it could not be a result of the work they have done. He is sure of that, but he has no idea how the problem might have originated. Worker B, on the other hand, agrees with

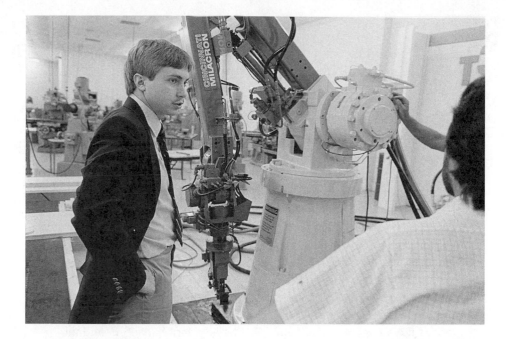

Worker A about the process and materials they have used at their stage of the assembly process, but he also asks several questions about such things as the carbon ratio in the steel as well as the cooling process of the parts before they get to the assembly line. The questions that Worker B asks lead you to follow up on those leads.

The result is that they find out that the source of incoming parts to your line has changed, and that indeed, the actual content of the steel is different. As it turns out, the problem did not originate at your stage of assembly, but occurred earlier, in the parts you were receiving. As a result of this discovery, which saves the company millions of dollars, you receive a promotion, and you must decide which worker will be promoted to replace you as supervisor of your line. Will you choose Worker A or Worker B?

Two students are reading from the same environmental science textbook. *(The reading is reproduced below.)*

Population Controls

Hunting for deer or other animals has become the target of a number of animal rights groups. At the same time, wolves and other large predators have become quite rare in most of the United States. Without predators to reduce their numbers, the deer populations in many Eastern states has grown rapidly. As a result, accidents involving deer being hit by automobiles have become quite common on rural roads. Deer are beginning to present a more serious problem for farmers and other home owners. If allowed to continue to multiply, they will with certainty begin to damage their own food supply and the result will be massive die-offs of deer in the wild.

The question is what is more desirable. Introducing predators into the wild and allowing them to survive would present a "natural" population control on the deer. The trade-off is that we must be willing to have large carnivorous predators in the forests before this solution will work.

Allowing increased hunting for deer would also provide a degree of population control. To accomplish this, hunting must be encouraged rather than discouraged. The trade-off is that many people believe that hunting is an inhumane activity that should not be encouraged at any cost.

The third solution is to allow the deer population to grow out of control. The trade-off will be the resulting damage to crops and gardens, increased accidents, and occasional massive deer die-offs from starvation and disease.

For every decision there are opportunity costs. There are always trade-offs in environmental issues.

Camp, William G., Ph.D. *Environmental Science For Agriculture and the Life Sciences*, (1994). Albany, New York: Delmar Publishers, Inc., pp. 36–37.

Both students learn that there are three solutions to controlling the deer population: reintroducing predators such as wolves, increasing hunting, or simply allowing the deer populations to grow unchecked.

When the class discussion gets to this topic, Student A has her mind made up. To her, hunting is a cruel and deplorable thing. She cannot picture herself or anyone else in her family shooting an animal. Student B, on the other hand, is not so sure, and has several questions for the teacher: what natural predators do deer have? Are wolves dangerous to humans? Are there other predators that hunt deer? How dangerous is hunting to humans? Which is more painful: starvation, bullets or attack by carnivores? How dangerous is it to the driver and passengers in a car when it runs into a deer? Could part of the solution be hunting and another part be the introduction of predators? Are some types of hunting more humane than others?

Student A (like Worker A in the previous example) is exhibiting behavior that is not characteristic of a good thinker. But, it is not that she does not care! In fact, she obviously feels very strongly about the situation and possible solutions (as Worker A also did with his situation.) Student B and Worker B in these two situations are better able to cope with the problems which they confront, not because they are more concerned nor because they are smarter. The difference is that they are able to use thinking skills better than their peers.

The SCANS Report

In April of 1992, the United States Department of Labor published the report of the *Secretary's Commission on Achieving Necessary Skills* (SCANS). This report outlines the necessary competencies needed for the future workplace. The information they gathered in this extensive study of business owners, managers, union officials, and line workers included not only job-specific skills, but also *thinking skills* which they described as "the ability to learn, to reason, to think creatively, to make decisions, and to solve problems," the same kinds of skills needed by those people you have just read about.

In this chapter we will show you why it is valuable to be able to think critically about something, and we will show you how to do it. We have also included several practices as well as a simple, easy to follow format to help you think better about anything you want, either in school or on the job. As the poem at the beginning of this chapter suggests, rehearsal and practice are just as important to thinking as they are to physical activities.

What is Critical Thinking?

Both students and company employees are often surprised when their teachers or managers ask them to do more than spit back facts. After all, that is usually the main task for students in elementary and high school classrooms. There is an old saying that a person can be "fact rich and idea poor." That is, a person can memorize and recall many facts about something he or she has read—main ideas, names, dates, places, paraphrasing situations and sequences of events—and still not *really know* what he or she has been reading. Reading for real understanding, like problem solving, requires more indepth thinking than the usual memorization of facts. Unfortunately, many students are not schooled in logical thinking strategies necessary for success in school or on the job.

To be a problem solver on the job or a successful student in college, a person must be able to read **more** than what is on the printed page. Whether reading a training manual for assembly line work or a college textbook, a good reader always uses strategies for effective thinking.

Critical thinking is not thinking negatively about something. Rather, it means ***thinking completely about*** something, being certain to judge all the implications of an idea. In so doing, a person goes beyond the most obvious to consider factors that are not evident at first. Will Brand X soap really clean better than other brands?...Does Ford really offer a quieter ride?...Do Democrats really represent the "working man?"...Should our government grant "most favored nation" status to a country whose government violates the civil rights of its people?...Is the problem with our welds in our process or something else?...Is hunting the best solution to overpopulation of deer? From simple buying decisions at the supermarket to complex questions about the ecosystem, **critical thinking**—judging the accuracy, worth, or validity of ideas or claims—is very important on the job, in the classroom, and in life. These skills are essential to being a good citizen and an effective adult in our society.

Thinking at Three Different Levels

To be able to think effectively or read effectively requires certain strategies. A critical thinker will move beyond the level of basic comprehension of facts to interpret and apply these facts.

Level One

You must first comprehend the *facts.* This is the *literal* level of understanding. Literal comprehension is important because it is the building block for all higher levels of understanding that might be required of you. So it is necessary that you understand the facts when you read.

Level Two

Another important ability is to see the relationships between and among the facts. This higher level of thinking is the key to *real* comprehension of reading material, and is called *interpretive comprehension.* It is important for you to see the larger ideas that come from relating the facts to each other. (Refer to Figure 6-1 to see how facts relate to each other to form one idea.) To do this you need to train yourself to differentiate facts from opinions and to judge **inferences**, hidden meanings that the author may have. You may often need to bring to bear your own past experiences and background to produce accurate interpretations. With some practice you can become adept at interpreting the author's point of view—even the biases or prejudices evident in the writing.

Adapted from Herber, H. (1978). *Teaching Reading In the Content Areas, 2nd Ed.* Englewood Cliffs, N.J.: Prentice-Hall.

Figure 6-1 Inferential Thinking: How Facts Relate to Meaning

Relating many facts can help you determine the author's real meaning. A person reading this chapter might see the relationship between 3 levels of thinking as facts A, B, and C in this diagram. All three combine to form the larger idea of complete thinking, fact D.

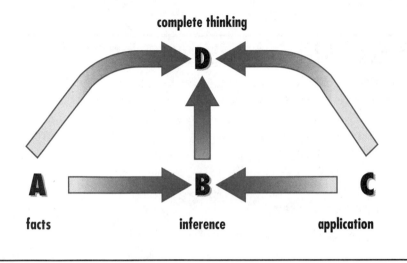

Level Three

The third level of thinking is knowing how to use the material; *being able to apply what you have read* to your own life or to other situations past, present or future is **application level thinking**. Common sense tells us that if we don't

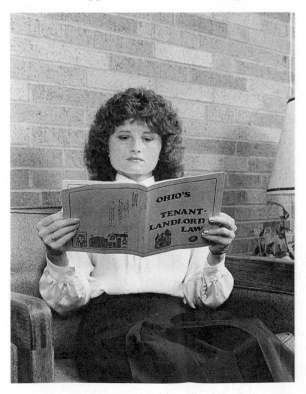

know how to use something we do not truly know or understand it. Also there is a good chance that we will soon forget material that we cannot apply. This high level of thinking is important because it keeps us from learning unrelated information in a vacuum—learned information has to fit together, and it has to be useful.

A C T I V I T Y 1 : **Thinking at Three Levels**

Now that you know about thinking at three levels, you can use the following activities to help you practice it. Read the following passage about how to handle a job interview. Then complete the post-reading exercise. It is all right to look back into the reading while you use the three-level study guide to help yourself think critically.

The Job Interview

Although each interview is a new experience, you need not be totally unprepared. Before the interview, learn as much as possible about the company and the job for which you are applying. Then, assess your career goals and objectives to see if your goals are consistent with those of the potential job. This kind of information indicates your interest and can help you formulate relevant questions.

Many employers ask about an applicant's immediate and long-range career goals. Employers also ask questions related to the applicant's background and qualifications. A review of your resumé will help you to prepare for such questions. Other questions may deal with your likes and dislikes, favorite classes, ability to work with others, ability to plan and manage your time and work, or reasons for choosing a certain occupation.

A typical job interview lasts 30 to 40 minutes. During that time, the interviewer will probably offer infor-

mation about the job and the company, ask questions, and give the applicant a chance to ask questions. You may be asked to complete an application form if you have not already done so.

When you interview for a job, answer each question precisely and honestly. Be sure you know how to pronounce both the name of the company and that of the interviewer. Using the name of the company or the interviewer whenever appropriate indicates interest and adds a personal touch to the interview. Ask questions that pertain to job duties and responsibilities, rather than to salary and fringe benefits. If the company is interested in hiring you, time will be provided to discuss salary and benefits. Also, you may need to ask about working hours, overtime work, tools, safety equipment, or certain procedures.

Although you do not want to appear too relaxed during the interview, you will want to appear confident and at ease. Avoid nervous mannerisms such as popping the knuckles, clearing the throat, twisting the hair, staring at the ceiling, or otherwise fidgeting. Such actions communicate a lack of interest or a lack of confidence. Do not chew gum or use any form of tobacco during the interview. Under no circumstances should you take anyone with you to the interview.

The employment interview is a special appointment. Shake hands with the interviewer before leaving. Handshaking is a common sign of good will among men and women. A neatly dressed, well-groomed applicant makes a good first impression. Wear appropriate, businesslike clothes, shoes, and accessories to the interview.

Toward the close of the interview try to determine what action will follow. It is not always possible to know your status a the end of an interview; but clarify what action, if any, you need to take after the interview. Will the interviewer notify you whether or not you are offered the job? When will a decision be made? Should you check with the employer at a later date? Does the interviewer need more information?

Kraska, Marie F. *Communication Skills for Trade and Industry,* (1985). Delmar Publishers, Inc., pp. 227–228.

Now use the study guide to help you to think about this reading.

T. Rogowski, © 1980.

Study Guide for *The Job Interview*

Place a check mark in the spaces next to statements with which you agree:

Literal Level Thinking

_____ **1.** You should prepare for a job interview by researching the company.

_____ **2.** Your career goals should include the kind of work for which you are applying.

_____ **3.** Always shake hands before and after the interview.

_____ **4.** You should answer all questions honestly.

_____ **5.** When you decide the interview is over, stand up and shake hands and leave.

Inference Level Thinking

_____ **6.** Each job interview you have may require a different set of questions you want to ask.

_____ **7.** One question employers often ask is what do you expect to be doing with your career five to ten years from now.

_____ **8.** It is best to "be yourself" at a job interview.

_____ **9.** Showing that you are interested in benefits to yourself such as salary and fringe benefits means you are a sharp person.

_____ **10.** You should leave knowing either that you have the job or what the next step is that either you ar the employer will take.

Application Level Thinking

_____ **11.** "You can always tell a person by his clothes."

_____ **12.** "Actions speak louder than words."

_____ **13.** "You can't judge a book by its cover."

_____ **14.** "The road of a thousand miles begins with a single step."

_____ **15.** If you don't get the job, you probably made some mistake in the interview.

The correctness of these statements is not as important as the process you used to think about them. (Your teacher may encourage a class discussion about these.) If you used this study guide carefully, it helped you to think at the three levels of literal, inferential, and application. With practice, you can think at these levels about anything, without using a study guide. You think about the facts, what they mean, and how they apply to real life. What happens when you think this way is more than meets the eye. First, you are encouraged to be more careful about what the reading really means. Unlike the "mulligan" exercise in chapter one, you are not just decoding the print to find answers. Instead, you are reading it to find meaning. You are also applying it to your own life and job interview situations. When we read words and think about not only what they mean, but also how they apply in the real world, we are becoming effective at thinking. And *reading is thinking*!

A C T I V I T Y 2 : More Thinking at Three Levels

Try another example from a Robert Frost poem:

The Road Not Taken

Two roads diverged in a yellow
    wood,
And sorry I could not travel both
And be one traveler, long I stood
And looked down one as far as
    I could
To where it bent in the under-
    growth;

Then took the other, as just as fair,
And having perhaps the better
    claim,
Because it was grassy and wanted
    wear;
Though as for that, the passing
    there
Had worn them really about the
    same.

And both that morning equally lay
In leaves no step had trodden
    black.
Oh, I kept the first for another day!
Yet knowing how way leads on to
    way,
I doubted if I should ever come
    back.

I shall be telling this with a sigh
Somewhere ages and ages hence:
Two roads diverged in a wood,
    and I —
I took the one less traveled by,
And that has made all the
    difference.

Lathem, Edward Connery, Ed. *The Poetry of Robert Frost, The Collected Poems, Complete and Unabridged,* (1969). New York: Henry Holt and Company, Inc., p. 105.

Study Guide for *The Road Not Taken*

Now, once again, check those statements with which you agree, using another way to think about the three levels of thinking when you are reading.

Right There on the Page:

____ **1.** The narrator is at a fork in the road, and has to decide whether to go to the left or to the right.

____ **2.** Only one of the two possible paths had been used prior to the time the narrator describes.

___ **3.** Both roads had been used before, and had about the same amount of traffic by others in the past.

___ **4.** The scene takes place in the summer on an unpaved path.

___ **5.** He took the road less traveled.

Reading Between the Lines:

___ **6.** If a person makes a wrong choice, he or she can always go back and start over again.

___ **7.** Regardless of which decision is made, there are certain decisions in life where a person may always wonder if the choice made was the better one.

___ **8.** The speaker in this poem is a nonconformist.

___ **9.** The narrator is pleased by his own life choices.

Reading Beyond the Lines:

___ **10.** Hindsight is 20/20.

___ **11.** A poem should "begin in delight and end in wisdom."

___ **12.** Doing what "everyone else" is doing is the easiest short term strategy, but may, in the long run, prove to have been foolhardy.

___ **13.** The highway of life has many forks in the road.

Remembering

Now you have practiced complete thinking twice. What you have done using these two examples of three level guides is what the more skilled worker, Worker B, and the more skilled student, Student B, had done previously. They were successful at problem solving because they knew how to think more completely about something. Another key benefit from thinking at three levels is that you remember much more of what you have read. Trying to remember facts when you have not thought about what they really mean and how they apply to the real world is like trying to memorize the phone book! Yet many students try to do that in school. The result is often poor grades and a sense of wondering why they are even in school.

If you practice thinking at three levels, you should see an increase in the level of understanding you achieve, and you should remember a great deal more. The results should be more enjoyment in school and higher grades.

Now take a reading from one of your own textbooks in any subject area, or one of the additional readings in the Appendix of this textbook, and use the format below to write down thoughts that describe the three levels of thinking. (You can be doing your homework at the same time!) On your own paper, take some notes from your reading. You can use the two-column note-taking format for this exercise.

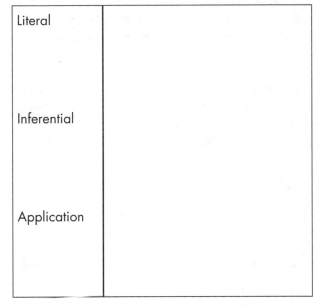

Consider the reading:

1. at the literal level. Jot down some key words or ideas from the reading you have chosen.
2. at the inferential level. Show how the facts relate. What does the author *mean?* What is/are the main idea(s)?
3. at the application level. Write about how what you have read means to you or other people or things in the real world.

The Importance of Notes

Now that you know about thinking at three levels, you should practice it with everything you learn or think about. Remember to start with the facts, think about how they relate, and how what you have learned applies in the real world. You can do this with readings, lectures, films, filmstrips, or any other form of learning. It helps to jot down some notes in the learning process so that you can go back and see how things relate to one another. That way you don't have to remember all the facts.

Super Thinking—Thinking at Six Levels

Have you ever had trouble thinking of what to write about in an essay, on a test or for homework? Here is a strategy that was designed as an activity to help people think about a topic before they write about it. It is also a way to improve the way you read and think.

Cubing

This technique is called **cubing** because you are encouraged to think of the six sides of a cube, each with a reminder of a higher level of thinking on it. Just as in using the three levels of thinking of factual, meaning, and application, the six sides of the cube start with simply describing what you are studying, and work through six steps all the way to the highest level of thinking, arguing about the topic. Psychologists suggest that when you are arguing about something, you are thinking at a very high level about it, yet using most or all of the lower levels of thinking to be successful. Cubing was developed by Courin and Corvan in their 1980 textbook entitled *Writing*.

Steps in Cubing

The six steps of this thinking procedure are as follows:

1. **Describe it.** What does it look like?

2. **Compare it.** You can compare it or contrast it to something else similar or different.

3. **Associate.** What does it make you think of? What comes to your mind when you think about the subject?

4. **Analyze it.** What is it made of? What are its component parts?

5. **Apply it.** How does it work? How does it function?

6. **Argue.** At this stage you either state reasons why it is good or bad or you tell reasons why it is important for us to know about it.

Figure 6-2 **The Thinking Cube**
A cube has six sides, and can remind you of the six levels of thinking.

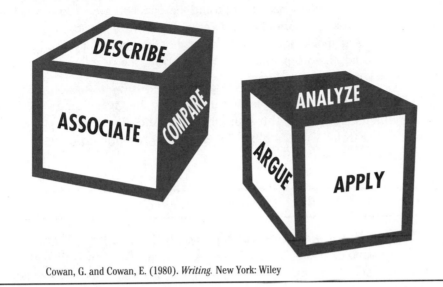

Cowan, G. and Cowan, E. (1980). *Writing*. New York: Wiley

Cubing a Pencil

A person can use this thinking strategy to think about anything from something as simple as a pencil to something as complex as the space shuttle program. Naturally, the more complex the thing or issue, the more thought that goes into it. Just for practice, lets "cube" a pencil. We will use each of the six steps above to do so.

Description: A pencil is a long, cylindrical (sometimes hexagonal), device used to write on paper.

Comparison: It is different than a pen because you can erase what you have written, which you cannot do with most pens.

Association: It makes me think of drawing because I like to draw with one. (It might make you think of just about anything, such as standardized tests or sharpening before class or your book bag. There is much room for personal thought at this level of thinking.)

Analysis: Pencils are generally made of wood surrounding and supporting a thin piece of graphite, which is the substance that marks the paper. It usually has a metal cylindrical clasp at the top which holds an eraser.

Apply: Once sharpened, it can be used by scraping the graphite part over the surface of the paper to write or draw. If you wish to make a correction, rub the rubber eraser on the paper to remove the graphite lines you made. When the graphite becomes dull, you may need to sharpen the pencil again.

Argue: An argument in favor of pencils is that they are an efficient tool for taking notes or writing a rough draft of something.

It is easy to make corrections if you make a mistake, simply by inverting the pencil and using the attached eraser to rub out the error. They are also lightweight and convenient to carry.

Arguments against pencils are that they frequently need sharpening, the graphite tips break too easily, the graphite gets all over my clothes, I always leave it at home, etc....

You can see from this example that using the cube gives you a simple structure which helps you to think about things. And, if you use this, you will never suffer from "writer's block," the inability to think about what to write in essays.

A C T I V I T Y 4 : Cubing

The wild African elephant faces extinction in the near future. Only 20,000 elephants of the 165,000 that were counted in Kenya fifteen years ago are still alive; 50,000 elephants in Tanzania have been killed within the past ten years. In Uganda, 90% of the elephants have been killed by poachers.

Why is this destruction occurring? Because poachers are killing elephants for their ivory tusks. The ivory is made into jewelry, which is sold all over the world. Would people buy this jewelry if they knew that elephants were a dying race?

Facts from The African Wildlife Association, (1988).

Now think about this reading by cubing it on your own paper.

1. **Describe the issue.**

2. **Compare it.** Does this issue remind you of a similar situation? How are they similar or different?

3. **Associate it.** What does it make you think of? Is there an incident or a feeling you get?

4. **Analyze the issue.** What are the parts of it?

5. **Apply it.** How does the situation occur? What might be done to solve this problem?

6. **Argue.** Take a stand. What are your opinions and the reasons for your stand?

Good Thinkers vs. Poor Thinkers

Thinking is to the brain like exercise is to the muscles. You need to exercise your mind by consciously thinking about things at levels that go beyond what meets the eye.

By using some simple rules, and by practicing, you can become a better thinker, a better reader, and a better student in school or worker on the job. By following some fairly simple steps you can think critically about things in school or on the job in such a way as to become a better problem solver. As Figure. 6-3 shows, good thinkers just think better, and you can see that by practicing thinking at different levels, you can help yourself to become one. As you can see from having done the previous activity, using the six levels of thinking really helps you to better understand a topic. Now try it with something you have either studied for homework or discussed in class. (Or even something else in your life. Cube your job. Cube your favorite sport. On your own paper, follow the six steps of cubing to write about the topic you have chosen. Describe, compare, associate, analyze, apply, argue.

Figure 6-3 Good Thinkers vs. Poor Thinkers

By using some simple rules and by practicing, you can become a better thinker, a better reader, and a better student.

Good Thinkers	Poor Thinkers
welcome problems and uncertain situations	look for black and white solutions, and avoid problems
try to look at all aspects of a problem, thinking methodically about alternatives	look for quick fix solutions that seem obvious
use different levels of thinking to analyze the situation methodically	give up quickly when correctness is not obvious
look for evidence to support their own ideas as well as opposing ideas	only look for evidence that supports what they already believe
ask "what if..." questions to apply apparent facts to the real world	fail to think at the application level, and only think at the literal level

SUMMARY

Critical thinking is a skill necessary to success in school, work, and life. Critical thinking means to think completely about something, being certain to consider and judge all the implications of an idea. This includes:

- thinking at the literal level of understanding.

- being able to interpret and infer.

- applying what you've read to your life and to the world.

Cubing involves six levels of thinking, in which you do the following: describe, compare, associate, analyze, apply, and argue.

WRITER'S WORKSHOP   On Your Own

As you can see from this chapter, using the six levels of thinking really helps you to better understand a topic. Now try it with something you have either studied for homework or discussed in class. Or use something else in your life. Cube your job. Cube your favorite sport. On your own paper, follow the six steps of cubing to write about the topic you have chosen. Describe, compare, associate, analyze, apply, argue.

FINAL CHECK

Circle the letter of the phrase that best completes the statement:

1. After I have read a chapter, it is a good idea to:
   a. underline the main idea.
   b. retell the main points of the whole chapter so that I can check to see if I understood it.
   c. read the chapter again to be sure I said all of the words correctly.
   d. practice reading the chapter aloud.

2. After I have read a chapter, it is a good idea to:
   a. read the title and look over the chapter to see what it is about.
   b. check to see if I have skipped any of the vocabulary words.
   c. think about how this information might relate to a specific situation.
   d. make a guess about what will happen in the next chapter.

3. After I have read a chapter, it is a good idea to:
   a. think about why this information is important.
   b. practice reading the chapter aloud.
   c. look over the chapter title and pictures to see what will happen.
   d. look at all the titles and subtitles.

Answers: 1. b; 2. c; 3. a

Strategies for More Effective Studying

CHAPTER 7

CHAPTER OBJECTIVES

After completing Chapter Seven, you will be able to:

- decide what speed is best for different types of reading.

- speed up your reading rate so you can read more material in the same time.

- use a note-taking system that helps you practice strategic reading and also makes studying easier and more effective.

- use several techniques that will help you to improve your memory.

Chapter Outline

I. Improving How You Do Your Studying

II. How to Improve Your Reading Speed

III. A Note-taking System That Helps You Read Better

IV. Improving Your Memory Ability

OPENING ACTIVITY

After previewing Chapter Seven, use the outline above to predict how you will accomplish each of the objectives listed. In your notebook, divide a page by drawing a line down the middle. The left side of the page will be for your predictions. You will write in this column before you read the chapter. For each objective, write down what you think you might be able to do to accomplish the goal. Then, on the right side, you can jot down notes you take as you read, right next to your predictions. (Remember from Chapter One that one of the best ways to learn something new is to make predictions about it, and then, see how your predictions differ from what you read.)

Improving How You Do Your Studying

Have you ever wondered why it seems so easy for some students to remember what they have read in their textbook or heard in a lecture? If you would like to improve your own ability to remember more, as well as to read faster and more effectively, then read on. Whether you are an "A" student or struggling in school, this chapter is important for you. The strategies in this chapter have been proven over the years to help students of all levels of ability and all levels of education, from elementary through graduate school, to study more efficiently, and get better grades.

It is important to mention up front that there is work involved in learning to study more effectively. You would not expect to read about how to improve your play in your favorite sport, and then go out on the playing field and find that you have become better at playing. You might be able to take what you have read about your sport and apply it in practice, and after much practice, become better at the sport. You will find the same to be true in the sport of studying. What you will learn in this chapter is how to improve your ability to use the three keys to success at studying:

1. Improving Your Reading Speed

2. Taking Effective Notes

3. Remembering What You Have Studied

It will be up to you to practice what you learn here.

"I took a speed-reading course, learning to read straight down the middle of the page, and I was able to read War And Peace *in 20 minutes. It is about Russia."*

WOODY ALLEN

How to Improve Your Reading Speed

The quote by comedian Woody Allen tells how many people feel about speed reading courses. Such courses guarantee to raise reading speed from 1,000 to 10,000 words per minute. Since most people read between 150-200 words per minute, it is not surprising that students and professionals from many fields take these courses. They all have hopes of being like the eleven-year-old girl

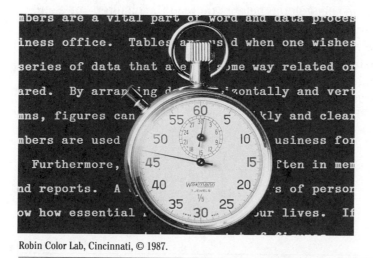

Robin Color Lab, Cincinnati, © 1987.

on the late night TV show who reads 40 pages of a novel in three minutes with total recall!

Different Speeds for Different Reads

Most of us cannot read with blazing speed and comprehend much of the material. There is hope, however, because the real trick to rapid reading is not how fast you read but how well you can read at faster speeds. It is of little use to read a book at 12,000 words per minute and not comprehend 90% of that book. The key to speeding up your reading speed, then, is *flexibility* in reading—adjusting your reading speed to suit the purpose for reading. Just as the driver of a car must adjust the speed of driving to meet the conditions of the road, the good reader must adjust the speed of reading to fit what is being read and the reason it is being read.

A C T I V I T Y   1 :   Your Reading Speeds

You will need a stopwatch or a clock with a second hand for this exercise. Read each of the following passages straight through, reading at a pace that allows you to understand it, and time yourself to see how long each one takes. (Time each one separately.)

Passage One:

Energy Sources

Most of our energy comes either directly or indirectly from the sun, the earth's most vital natural resource. Capturing the energy that begins in the sun has always been our greatest challenge.

Over the centuries we have used the force of moving air, the wind, to move our goods and to pull water from the earth. Windmills once dotted the American landscape. Sailing ships crossed the oceans and great lakes of the world. We cannot compare the quantity of wind in the past to that today. Neither can we conserve nor waste wind. We can only use it whenever possible and try to keep it clean. With the energy crisis of the 1970's there was a growing interest in the use of wind power. Then the energy "glut" of the 1980's lowered the interest in wind power.

Another great energy source is coal. It is probably the most widely distributed storehouse of the sun's energy. Coal was first discovered in America in 1673, in what is now Illinois. In 1824 about 81,000 tons of coal were mined in this country. By 1947 that figure had grown to 676 million tons. Although the amount of coal mined has declined over the last two decades, a total of 35 billion tons has been produced in the United States since mining began. ...

Camp, William G., and Dougherty, Thomas B., and Kirts, Carla. *Managing Our Natural Resources,* (1991). New York: Delmar.

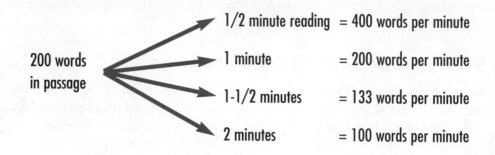

200 words
in passage

1/2 minute reading = 400 words per minute

1 minute = 200 words per minute

1-1/2 minutes = 133 words per minute

2 minutes = 100 words per minute

Now read this second passage, and once again time yourself.

Passage Two:

Laws Requiring Clear and Complete Disclosure of Terms in Loans and Credit Sales

A consumer loan arises when a person borrows money primarily for personal, family, household, or agricultural purposes. It is often called a personal loan to distinguish it from a business or commercial loan.

By requiring complete and clear disclosure of loan terms, the federal Truth in Lending Act (which is part of the Consumer Credit Protection Act) best exemplifies laws designed to protect consumers when they become debtors. In particular, it requires creditors to furnish debtors with certain information. This law does not limit the percentage amounts that may be charged. However, creditors must make a full disclosure of interest and finance charges whenever the consumer loan is repayable in four or more installments or carries a finance charge. The **finance charge** is the total added cost when one pays in installments for goods or services. The creditor must also declare the true equivalent annual interest rate or annual percentage rate (APR). Thus, 1-1/2 percent a month must be stated as 18 percent a year. Under the law, a credit sales contract must also state such details as the cash price of the item; the down payment or trade-in allowance, if any; an itemized list of finance charges; and the total amount to be financed. In the problem, Reliable Finance is obligated to tell the (customers) the total cost....

Mietus, Norbert J. and Adamson, John E. and Conry, Edward J. *Law For Business,* (1993). Cincinnati, OH: South-Western.

The chances are that, unless you are an expert at consumer loans and business law, the second passage took a bit longer to read, even though it had approximately the same number of words as the first. The reason for this difference is that most people read much faster when reading things about which they know more, and they also read more rapidly when reading material in which they are interested. Most high school students would probably know more about energy sources than about consumer loans.

This activity illustrates that there are different levels of reading. The fact is that there are four levels of reading, as follows:

Level of Reading	Example	Purpose	Speed Range
1. Slow/systematic	highly technical text, poetry	careful analysis & evaluation	100-200 wpm
2. Studying	textbooks	comprehension and recall	200-300 wpm
3. Bold reading	novels newspapers	comprehension to bring enjoyment	300-500 wpm
4. Rapid reading	novels newspapers magazines reference materials	overviews skimming scanning	500-1000 wpm

Just knowing that there are different rates for different types of reading can help you to read better. By knowing what type of reading you are preparing to do, you can help yourself by judging how fast you should proceed. You should also recognize that you can, with practice, speed up the rate at which you read all of these types of material.

©1981 Universal Press Syndicate

"I want a book on speed-reading and 85 Westerns."

Practicing to Improve Reading Speed

The factors that affect speed are difficulty of the material being read, fear of missing something, and technique (how you move your eyes on the page).

Difficulty. The first and most obvious roadblock to faster reading is the difficulty of the material being read. Sometimes material is difficult because you don't have a background of experience sufficient enough for familiarity with the material. All of us have heard someone say after telling a particularly bad joke, "Well, I guess you had to be there!" In a real sense a person has to have "been there—experienced what it is that is being read. Lack of experience will cause the material to seem more difficult and demanding. One way to help yourself along these lines is to always use the previewing procedure described in Chapter Two. Textbook authors select photographs and charts and graphs that help the reader make sense of their work. Failure to use these valuable clues will handicap your reading.

Fear of Missing Something. Most of us have been trained from childhood to read slowly and carefully so we don't miss anything. The result is that many persons read at about the speed at which they can talk—about 125 words per minute. They say the words to themselves while reading. This is called "subvocalizing." This is a very inefficient and wasteful way to read. Though we can never entirely stop subvocalizing, we can read much more rapidly by limiting such inner speech to 30-40% of what is read. To speed up and subvocalize less, the reader needs to focus on *phrase units*, or groups of words. You may be surprised to learn that it takes no longer to read phrase units than it does to read individual letters or single words. Take the test on the next page by timing yourself or having someone time you on reading down first column A, then column B, then column C:

A	B	C
r	life	Sometime later
t	stem	I am resting
b	flow	peacefully
v	test	and the wind
m	same	still blows steadily,
q	book	
l	that	and I find myself
a	them	attentive and enraptured.
f	moan	There, from
h	bash	my window
p	such	I watch
c	home	this cold wind
j	wake	cross the road
o	hold	and slam the trees.
u	roam	The blowing branches
d	sides	
i	lept	are illuminated
w	sock	by moonlight, and
y	shin	cause me to reflect
e	term	on my limited time.
k	take	
seconds	seconds	seconds
21 letters	21 words	49 words

Chances are there was very little, if any, difference in the reading time for the three columns. Our minds are like computers which are fine-tuned to process much information at a rapid pace. The key is—don't be afraid of missing something. Relax and consciously read faster through the phrase reading technique and you probably won't miss anything. In fact comprehension should be improved!

Technique. The eye movement techniques described here in practicing phrase reading will help you read much more rapidly. It will require practice of 15 to 30 minutes every day if you wish to get really good, but it will get easier each day. Also, your comprehension may decrease a bit in the beginning. But with practice, you will soon be reading faster and your comprehension will slowly improve to an adequate level. (Remember to preview the reading to help in comprehension.)

1. **Practice phrase reading** by swinging the eyes across the page stopping only every few words. Try this:

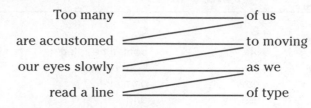

Too many ———————— of us
are accustomed ———————— to moving
our eyes slowly ———————— as we
read a line ———————— of type

2. **Don't go back over what you have read.** Everyone does this without really thinking about it when it is happening. These backward and upward movements are called regressions. Obviously, the fewer regressions one makes the faster the material can be read.

3. **Consciously move faster.** During the 10-30 minutes of practice each day, read faster than normal and comfortable. Do not be afraid of missing something being read. A good exercise is a three minute "mental push-up." This is accomplished by reading faster than normal for 3 minutes, then closing the book and jotting down people, places and things that you noticed. Then go back over the same material for a second (and even third if necessary) three minute push-up, each time jotting down more of what is remembered.

4. **Anticipate what is coming.** The sense of the sentence will often telegraph whole words instantly, just from their first syllable or two. This is because the "drift" of the sentence signals what the word must be. By anticipating the author's line of reasoning, speed of reading will be increased.

5. **Decrease dependence on subvocalization.** Subvocalization was mentioned earlier. When this is reduced, rate of reading becomes more rapid. This "inner speech" is a roadblock that will limit reading to nearly the speed at which we talk—about 125 words per minute. To reduce subvocalization, you must take the word directly from the eye to the brain. With practice you can do it!

6. **Pace yourself with a tracking device.** A finger pacing technique can be used to help concentrate and practice phrase reading. Begin with the finger one-fourth of the way through the line and lightly touch it down on the page four times. Try to get a rhythm going by the phrase reading method described in step 1, above. You should be trying to read four or five phrases on each line, expanding the horizontal line of vision in the following manner:

Figure 7-2 Finger motion when phrase reading

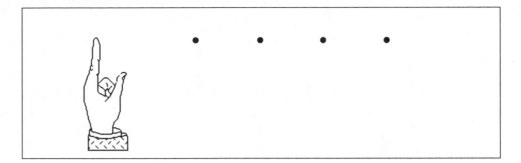

As reading becomes more rapid, you may wish to make only two or three fixations per line. Your finger may be swept in a short curving motion to take in more than one line at a time. In this manner you will begin to use more vertical peripheral vision so you can see more than one line at a time: This is illustrated in the following manner:

Figure 7-3 Finger motion for more rapid reading

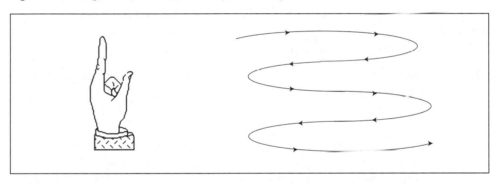

After several months of practice using the above method, you will probably be able to shift into high gear on occasion, using a vertical tracking method. In this technique, you go down the middle of the page, keeping the finger in the middle, making only two fixations of your eyes per line or per several lines. This, however, is for experienced rapid readers and should be kept in mind as an ultimate goal of rapid reading practice.

Figure 7-4 Finger Motion for Vertical Tracking

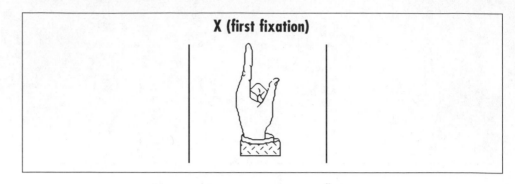

X (first fixation)

A C T I V I T Y 3 : Practice That Is Fun

An enjoyable way to practice rapid reading is to find books that you are interested in and enjoy. This allows you to have the pleasure of reading something
that **you want to** read, rather than just reading assigned readings from school.
Ideally, you should get a novel or biography of interest to you that you really
want to read. Then you can use the form in Figure 7-5 to time yourself. If you
practice this way, you will be able to see your own reading speed increase in
just a few days. These are the steps you should follow:

1. After selecting a book you like, count the words on an average page. Record
   that number in the space labeled "words per page."

2. Set a timer for five minutes.

3. Practice reading at your normal pace the first time. When the five minutes is
   up, count the number of pages you have read, dividing partial pages into
   fractions, such as tenths of a page. Enter that number in the space labeled
   "pages read."

4. Simply multiply the number of words per page times the pages read in the
   time allowed to find your reading rate.

5. Once you have done this for your normal rate, you may begin to apply the
   rapid reading techniques described above. Use the same formula to measure
   your progress through the book. You will see progress almost instantly! And
   you will continue to get better.

The best part of this is that you are reading something of interest to you
to improve your speed, but the practice will carry over into your schoolwork.
All your reading will get easier and faster.

Figure 7-5 Reading Rate Calculator

Reading Rate Report

Materials needed: Stopwatch or watch with timer, an interesting book.

Date _____

Title of Book _____

Words per page _____

Pages/5 minutes _____

Number of words per 5 minutes _____
$$(\text{wpp} \times \text{pages}/5)$$

A Note-taking System That Helps You Read Better

We have already mentioned the two-column note-taking system in Chapter Five. This section of the chapter will describe a reading plan that you can use with two-column notes so that you will improve your comprehension the first time through the reading, **and** you will have such good quality notes that you should not have to go back into the textbook to study for tests. Your notes are all that you will need!

Hyde Park Branch, Public Library of Cincinnati & Hamilton Co., © 1987.

Two-Column Note-taking

Two-column notes are a way to separate the main ideas from details, always keeping the main topic on the left side of the page as shown in Figure 7-6.

Students who use two-column notes in all their classes for both class notes and reading notes report much greater ease in remembering information for tests and better understanding of the courses they take.

Figure 7-6 Two-Column Notes

CHAPTER 6 OBJECTIVES	1. Define critical thinking & why imp. 2. Describe thinking at 3 levels. 3. Thinking at six levels.		
"WORD FOCUS"	REALLY KNOW thinking	A LITTLE critical thinking application analyzing	DON'T KNOW inferential cubing literal level
What is critical thinking?	Thinking <u>completely</u> about something (like assembly line worker and environmental student)		
What are 3 levels of thinking? like the 3-level guide	1. LITERAL – the facts: what is actually there in the reading 2. INFERENCE – where <u>you interpret</u> the author's <u>meaning</u>. (reading between the lines) 3. APPLICATION – where you apply it to the real world. (You think about what it means to you.)		
How can you think at 6 levels?	CUBING: (6 sides on a cube) helps you to think at six increasingly higher levels — Describe, Compare, Associate, Analyze, Apply, Argue. 1st describe: What's it look like? 2nd associate: What do you think of?		

PQR$_2$ST+: Reading Notes for Successful Studying

Many students do not know how to take notes when they are reading. As a result, they often don't take them at all. But reading notes can be very useful. If you have good reading notes, you will usually not have to go back and study the textbook before tests and quizzes. Taking good reading notes also means better understanding of the reading the first time through.

We have designed and tested a note-taking system that is very effective. The letters in the name PQR$_2$ST+ stand for **P**review, **Q**uestion, **R**ead & **R**emember, **S**can, and **T**ouch up. To see how you might use this system, each of these is outlined in more detail below:

Preview: This is a very important step that good readers always do. It involves a quick overview of the material to be read before starting to read. Chapter 1 details this procedure, but to review, these are the things to look for in the preview:

- title
- introduction
- subtitles
- pictures
- charts, maps, graphs
- bold print and italicized words
- summary
- review questions

Question: In the left column of a page formatted for two-column notes, write the question or objective which you hope to achieve. A great way to do this is to turn the subtitle of a passage into a question. For example, if, in a chapter on the internal combustion gasoline engine, the subtitle of the reading is "THE CAMSHAFT," you might, before reading, write in your left column, "What is a camshaft?" The next step is...

Read: Here, you simply read the subsection silently, while you think about how you are going to put the information **in your own words**. The next step is...

Remember: In the right column of the notes, **WITH THE BOOK CLOSED**, you write down the details of what you have read. This must be in your own words! Do your best to recall as much as possible in your notes, but do not worry about missing some details, because the next step is...

Scan: You now go back over the same subsection of the text in a very rapid scan to see if you have missed any details that are important, or if you have gotten anything wrong in your notes. Then...

Touch Up: Add any important details to your notes at this time.

+(Plus): The last step should be done within the first 24 hours of the reading. That is to go back and study from the notes by folding the page so that only the question part shows. See if you can remember the details on the right side. You will see that because of the way you took these notes, you are able to recall important details that you used to forget with your old study system. Go over the notes again before the test and see if your grades don't improve. (Figure 7-6 shows what PQR$_2$ST+ notes might look like for a segment of Chapter 6 of this book.)

The reason that this system is so powerful is that by forcing yourself to take the notes with the book closed, you are making yourself do a better job of reading in the first place. (Whenever you make yourself comprehend well enough to be able to summarize a passage in your own words, you are using the best process of reading.) And by going back in for the quick scan for missed details, you train yourself to read faster, while you are making certain that your notes are of top quality. **The result is that you can study from a few pages of quality notes rather than having to go back over pages and pages of textbook material.**

A C T I V I T Y   4 :   Application to This Textbook

Try reading the last section of this chapter on memory ability, using the PQR$_2$ST+ method of reading and note-taking. Be sure to follow the steps of previewing, questioning (in the left column), reading & remembering (in the right column), scanning for missed details, and touching up your notes. Then before your next class, read your notes over, trying to remember the right side details while covering them up. Doing this will make you well prepared for your next class.

Improving Your Memory Ability

Hopefully, using the reading/note-taking technique of PQR$_2$ST+ will be a great aid in recalling facts and details for tests, writings, and other activities in class. But, have you ever wondered why it is hard to remember what we have heard in a lecture, on a film, or in a reading? The answer is... *It is natural to forget!*

Almost a hundred years ago, an Austrian psychologist named Hermann Ebbinghaus conducted an exhaustive study involving himself and many other people of his village over a fourteen year period. He studied the task of remembering lists of items, some of which were short, and some longer. For years, he painstakingly recorded the observations he collected. The results can be shown in this "curve of forgetting":

Figure 7-7 The Ebbinghaus Curve of Forgetting

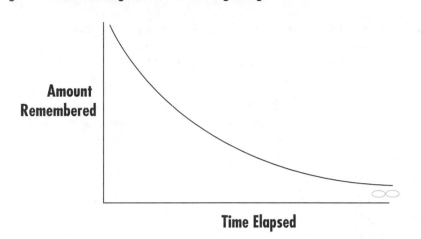

He found that within a twenty minute period, a person is likely to forget approximately 47% of what he has learned. Within one day, that grows to 62%, and, within two weeks, it grows to about 80%! No wonder students sometimes have difficulty passing tests!

Techniques for Helping You to Remember

One thing we can learn from the work of Ebbinghaus is certain: "one shot" reading-study sessions will not insure learned material will be retained for any length of time. To study and retain material takes hard work and the use of certain techniques for remembering.

1. **Converting Short Term Memory to Long Term Memory.** When you study, information bombards the brain through the eyes, ears, and sometimes, your touch (if you are taking notes.) All the information is viewed and either discarded or stored in a temporary memory system called *short term memory*. To transfer information from short term memory into permanent, or *long term memory*, the brain has to perform several functions. First, the brain has to decide that the information is important enough. If all information in short term memory were "pushed" over into long term memory, a phenomenon would occur called *information overload*. To prevent this, the brain makes selections, committing to permanent memory only those items it deems are absolutely necessary to retain.

    If the information is important and needs to be stored, one has to perform a certain task to assure this: ***reciting***. By learning the material over and over in our minds, we are helping to transfer the information from short term memory to long term memory. We help ourselves transfer the information by the reciting process by repeating the information, or by summarizing the information. (You can understand why the PQR_2ST+ process is so successful. It not only prepares you to read, but it helps you

> *The art of remembering is the art of thinking; . . . when we wish to fix a new thing in . . . our . . . mind . . . our conscious effort should not be so much to impress and retain it as to connect it with something else already there. The connecting is the thinking; and if we attend clearly to the connection, the connected thing will certainly be likely to remain within recall.*
>
> WILLIAM JAMES
> TALKS TO TEACHERS ON
> PSYCHOLOGY

push information to long term memory by both summarization and repetition.)

2. **Chunking Bits of Information.** The chunking of large amounts of information into categories can help you remember information more readily and retrieve information faster. For instance, suppose you had to learn these concepts in a social studies class:

tools	minerals	water
labor	machinery	power plants
trees	capital resources	manpower
wildlife	factories	natural resources
human resources	tractors	typewriters

These 15 concepts would be difficult to learn and remember. If you divided the different concepts into groups and labeled the first group *natural resources*, the second *capital resources*, and the third *human resources*, you would be practicing "chunking" of information into categories. These could be held in short term memory long enough for you to push them (by reciting) into long term memory. The groups would look like this:

Natural Resources	**Capital Resources**	**Human Resources**
minerals	tools	labor
water	machinery	manpower
trees	factories	
wildlife	tractors	
	typewriters	
	power plants	

If you stop reading often enough to review and to categorize information in this manner you will be better able at the completion of the reading to recite the information to yourself. (The use of two-column notes helps you to chunk by labeling main ideas on the left side, and listing detailed information on the right!)

3. **Mnemonic Devices.** Mnemonic (pronounced with a silent M) is a Greek term which means "bringing to mind." Using mnemonic aids can help you bring large quantities of information to your mind.

a. **Rhymes.** Rhyming words are used to aid in remembering.

Thirty days hath September, April, June, and November....

In fourteen hundred ninety-two, Columbus sailed the ocean blue.

b. **Acronyms.** In this device, the first letters in each word of a jingle, saying, or sentence either spell or remind you of the list to be memorized.

ROY G. BIV—the color spectrum: **R**ed, **O**range, **Y**ellow, **G**reen, **B**lue, **I**ndigo, **V**iolet.

HOMES—the great lakes: **H**uron, **O**ntario, **M**ichigan, **E**rie, **S**uperior.

PQR$_2$ST+—the study system: **P**review, **Q**uestion, **R**ead/Remember, **S**can, **T**ouch-up, **P**lus study your notes.

Acronyms can be made for any information necessary to recall. To improve our reading-study skills, for example, we could say "RELAX" by doing the following:

Rest plenty.
Exude enthusiasm.
Laugh often.
Anticipate what's coming.
Xcite yourself about the reading.

‹. **Association by Image.** This can be one of the most valuable ways of remembering lengthy lists of names, and relationships. One of the authors taught his students how to remember the names and positions of the 23 cabinet level officers in the President's service, all in one 50 minute class. All the students got an "A" on the quiz that day, and with a bit of rehearsal, again the following day. By the third day, all students knew the whole list for good! Here's how:

Students were taught to come up with "way out" associations between the names of the cabinet officers and their cabinet positions. For instance, one year, the Secretary of the Interior was a man named Donald Hodel. Students said, "When I think of a hotel, I think of a plush interior." When the Transportation Secretary was named Skinner, students said, "If you were transporting products, and you fell out the back of the truck you would probably get skinned when you hit the road surface." As outlandish as these may seem, they help the mind to make visual images that relate the name with the position. Similarly, any lengthy list of names or other pieces of information can be easily committed to memory.

Remember, though, that these mnemonic devices have limited usefulness because they don't deal with understanding what has been read. Also, these devices are an aid to short-term memory for retrieval at a much later date. You need to be cautious about over-reliance on these techniques. The more complete and effective way ***to read for thorough understanding*** is to apply ***chunking strategies***, and use systematic ***rehearsal*** through **PQR$_2$ST+**.

S U M M A R Y

By working to improve your reading speed, taking better quality notes when you read, and practicing memory techniques, you will increase your skill in reading, learning, and studying. The key to improved reading speed is flexibility—adjusting your reading speed to suit the type of material and your purpose for reading. The factors that affect reading speed are (1) the difficulty of the material, (2) fear of missing something, and (3) how you move your eyes on the page.

Note-taking systems can also help you read and study more effectively. Two-column notes and the PQR$_2$ST+ system go hand-in-hand as a study system, including the following steps:

- preview

- question

- read

- remember

- scan

- touch up

- plus (a review of your notes within the first 24 hours)

Memory devices, such as reciting, chunking, rhymes, acronyms, and association by image, are also effective study aids.

WRITER'S WORKSHOP

Try using the PQR$_2$ST+ system of reading and note-taking on the reading on pages 119-121, from a book on business and the economy: Be sure to refer to the steps listed in this chapter, being careful not to leave any out. Begin by setting up your note paper for taking two-column notes, placing a line 1/3 the way across the page. Then start your preview. (Refer to the steps of previewing, above.) If you wish to substitute another textbook or manual, feel free to do so. The sooner you practice, and the more you practice, the quicker you will see the value of this procedure.

WHAT IS A SMALL BUSINESS?

When we use the term **small business**, we are referring to a business that:

- Usually has the owner as the manager.
- Is not dominant in its field of operation.
- Employs fewer than 500 people.
- Usually is local, serving the nearby community.

You may be surprised that a small business may employ up to 500 people. However, businesses with only one to four employees are a major factor in our work force. Figure 14-2 shows that more than half of the employees of private business firms are employed in businesses that have four or fewer employees.

Figure 14-2
Small businesses employ the greatest percentage of employees in private businesses.

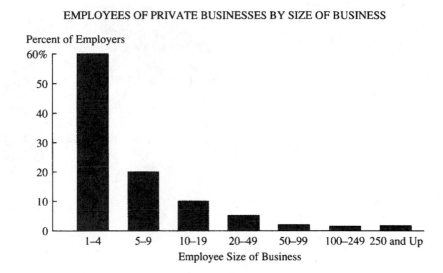

EMPLOYEES OF PRIVATE BUSINESSES BY SIZE OF BUSINESS

Source: National Federation of Independent Business, Research and Education Foundation, *Small Business Primer* (1988), 5.

Most small businesses begin as sole proprietorships. It is not unusual, however, for a person to begin his or her own business through a franchise agreement (see Chapter 6). Many small businesses eventually become incorporated. The advantages of a corporation, as pointed out in Chapter 6, are reasons why some small-business owners decide to incorporate their businesses. The most common form of ownership for small businesses, however, continues to be the sole proprietorship.

Our government has an agency set up to help small businesses; it is called the **Small Business Administration (SBA)**. The SBA is a government-funded organization that helps small-business owners borrow money as well as manage their businesses more efficiently. Information about the SBA and

(Continued on the following page)

its services can be obtained by contacting an office in your city or state or by writing to the SBA, 1441 L Street, Washington, DC 20416.

Small businesses are found in all of the industries you learned about in Chapter 8. A recent analysis showed that the largest percentage of small businesses are found in retailing—28 percent—and in services—24 percent (see Figure 14-3). Courtney's new business venture would place her in the services industry.

Figure 14-3
The largest percentage of small businesses are found in retailing and services.

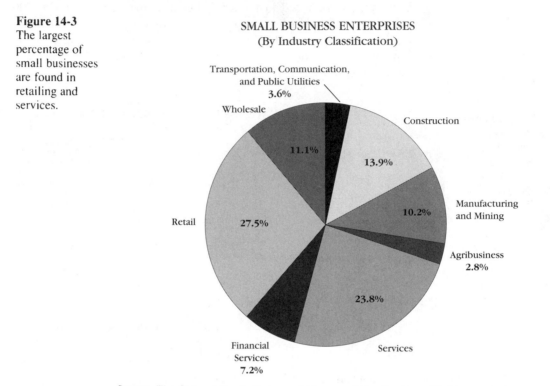

SMALL BUSINESS ENTERPRISES
(By Industry Classification)

Source: *The State of Small Business: A Report of the President* (Washington, D.C.: U.S. Government Printing Office, 1989).

Some businesses are classified as venture businesses. A **venture business** is one that has been in operation for less than three years and has no employees other than the owner. In one year, more than 1,600 new venture businesses were started every day in the United States. Courtney would operate of those 1,600 venture businesses.

HOW SUCCESSFUL ARE SMALL BUSINESSES?

Small businesses make many contributions to our economy as innovators of new products and developers of new production processes. Small businesses adjust more quickly to changing market demands than do large businesses. They can experiment with new products and new methods of production without waiting for approval from management committees.

Not all small businesses succeed; in fact, their failure rate is quite high. Figure 14-4 shows the number of business closings due to bankruptcies and failures for the period from 1981 through 1987. A **bankruptcy** is a situation in which a business does not have enough money to pay its creditors even after selling its equipment and other capital resources. A **creditor** is a person or business that is owed money. A **failure** is the closing of a business with a loss occurring to at least one creditor. Although these figures represent a small percentage of small businesses, the number of failures is of some concern. In addition to these official figures, some small enterprises just quietly go out of business when the owner believes that he or she is not doing well enough to continue.

Figure 14-4
Small businesses close because of bankruptcies and failures.

Business Closings, 1981-1987

Year	Bankruptcies	Failures	Total
1981	48,086	17,044	65,130
1982	69,242	25,346	94,588
1983	62,412	31,334	93,746
1984	64,211	52,078	116,289
1985	81,277	57,067	128,344
1986	80,400	61,601	142,001
1987	60,828*	61,236	122,064*

* Only the first nine months of 1987 are included.

Source: *The State of Small Business: A Report of the President* (Washington, D.C.: U.S. Government Printing Office, 1988), 25.

WHY SMALL BUSINESSES FAIL

In a typical year, more than half of the businesses that fail have been in operation less than five years and are classified as small businesses. The reasons for failure are quite varied. The following are the most common reasons for failure:

- Not keeping adequate records.
- Not having enough start-up money.
- Lack of sales and management experience.
- Lack of experience with the type of business.
- Not controlling operating expenses.
- Poor location for the business.
- Failure to manage payments due from customers for purchases made.

Introduction to Business, The Economy and You. Cincinnati, OH: South-Western, p. 200-202.

FINAL CHECK

Circle the letter of the phrase that best completes the statement. (Answers follow.)

1. Before I begin reading, it is a good idea to:
   a. retell all of the main points that have happened so far.
   b. ask myself questions that I would like answered in the chapter.
   c. think about the meanings of the words which have more than one meaning.
   d. look through the chapter to find all of the words with three or more syllables.

2. While I am reading a chapter, it is a good idea to:
   a. stop to retell the main points to see if I am understanding what has happened so far.
   b. read the chapter quickly so I can find out what happened.
   c. read only the beginning and end of the chapter to find out what it is about.
   d. skip the parts that are too difficult for me.

3. After I have read a chapter, it is a good idea to:
   a. count how many pages I read with no mistakes.
   b. check to see if there were enough pictures to go with the chapter to make it interesting.
   c. check to see if I met my purpose for reading the chapter.
   d. immediately answer the questions provided at the end of the chapter.

Answers: 1. b; 2. a; 3. c

How to Overcome Difficult Words

CHAPTER OBJECTIVES

After completing Chapter Eight, you will be able to:

- understand why knowing words is so important to reading comprehension.

- learn how to add depth to your understanding of words.

- learn that motivation and attitude are important to learning technical and unfamiliar words.

- learn ways to remember new words.

- learn a vocabulary study system to help you master difficult reading material.

Chapter Outline

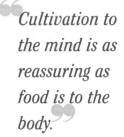

Cultivation to the mind is as reassuring as food is to the body.

CICERO

OPENING ACTIVITY

How do you learn new and unfamiliar vocabulary terms and words when you come upon them in your reading? Do you skip over them? Do you have a system for learning unfamiliar words, such as sounding them out? Do you consult a dictionary when encountering an unfamiliar word in your reading? Take a minute and jot down some strategies you have for learning unfamiliar words. Perhaps you can share these with classmates or with the whole class.

The Importance of Words in Reading

Read the following paragraph and think about the beautiful way that Annie Dillard uses words and language.

> This is it, I think, this is it, right now, the present, this empty gas station, here, this western wind, this tang of coffee on the tongue, and I am patting the puppy, I am watching the mountain. And the second I verbalize this awareness in my brain, I cease to see the mountain or feel the puppy. I am *opaque*, so much black asphalt. But at the same second, the second I know I've lost it, I also realize that the puppy is still squirming on his back under my hand. Nothing has changed for him. He draws his legs down to stretch the skin out so he feels every fingertip's stroke along his furred and arching side, his flank, his flung-back throat.

Dillard, Annie, *Pilgrim at Tinker Creek*, (1974). New York: Harper & Row.

Words are important for you to know and use effectively for success in life. If you never get past saying "W'sup, dude?" you unfortunately (and erroneously) may be perceived as less intelligent. A powerful vocabulary makes others take note of you and take an interest in you. This is reason enough to learn new words. Another reason is that learning new words helps in reading comprehension which will bring better success in school and in life.

For success in school, work and life, you need to increase your vocabulary knowledge. If you are staggered by the thought of having to learn even a few hundred new words a year—and well you might be, since many people add as few as 25 new words per year—please be assured that it is not an impossible task. But, before you begin the task, there are some things you should know about word knowledge.

Remember when you read the "golfer" passage in Chapter 1? Did you have trouble because you were unfamiliar with the specialized meanings of seemingly simple words such as "drop," "carpet," "gimme" and "leather"? That is because words can have both a surface meaning (drop a golf ball on the ground) and a deep meaning (a drop represents a free golf stroke without

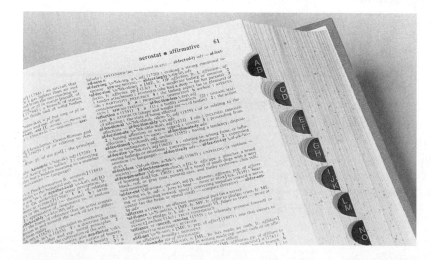

penalty). This is often called **surface structure** and **deep structure** of language.

In the *Pilgrim at Tinker Creek* passage, "opaque" means not reflecting or emitting light. Yet the word can have a deep structure that means more than simply not able to reflect light. The word can bring out all the feelings we have when we daydream, wander aimlessly off the subject, or simply forget. It is a powerful word that might mean different things to different people.

Unfamiliar words, whether it be ones you have never encountered before or ones with specialized meanings, will slow your ability to comprehend if you do not know their deep meaning. Therefore, you will need to be careful how you approach unfamiliar words when you meet them in your study and technical reading.

An informal study was conducted to find out what strategies college freshmen use to attack unfamiliar words in reading. The overwhelming majority of those sampled said that they simply skipped over unfamiliar words. While this strategy may work in some situations, it is a dangerous habit. If too many words are skipped, understanding at the deep level is not achieved. While skipping words may work for you in the short run, it is not a habit that will motivate you to learn better. Motivation is needed to push yourself to learn new words.

Words are things; and a small drop of ink, falling like dew upon a thought, produces that which makes thousands, perhaps millions, think.

GEORGE GORDON
LORD BYRON

Learning Through the Context of the Passage

Think of any word in isolation; then try to define that word. Let's take the word *run*, for instance. It is not difficult to give a synonym for the word, but it does not have an absolute meaning until it is placed in context. You may have immediately thought of the most common definition, "to move with haste," but anyone who would define run as "to be or campaign as a candidate for election" or "to publish, print, or make copies," or even "to cause the stitches in a garment to unravel" would have been equally accurate. The most exact meaning cannot be determined until the word is placed in context.

Read the following sentence:

The *unmistakable* conclusion, *bolstered* by much expert testimony in court, seems to *vindicate* the man in naming her as the killer.

What does *unmistakable* mean? How do the words "*bolstered* by much expert testimony in court..." help us figure out what *vindicate* means? What does *vindicate* mean? How does context help you to figure out the meanings of these words? Using surrounding words to figure out a word's meaning is one of the easiest and best ways to learn new words. The method is called *using context* to discover the meaning of words.

Following are some ways to discover the meanings of words through context.

1. **Definition** – You can often find a definition for a word within the sentence where it's used. This technique is used frequently in textbooks when an author introduces terminology. Note the following example:

   Oxidation, the combining of alcohol with oxygen in the tissues, begins in the liver where alcohol is changed at a constant rate to a toxic chemical.

2. **Signal Words** – Words or phrases may be used to signal the reader that a word or term is about to be explained or that an example will be presented. Some of the most frequently used signal words are listed below, followed by two example sentences using signal words.

like	the way	such
this	in the way that	such as
these (synonym)	for example	especially

   Americans do need to fear *hyperinflation*, especially as it involves prices rising at a very rapid rate.

   The individual may be influenced by other *agencies of socialization* such as religious groups, Boy Scouts and Girl Scouts, and youth organizations.

3. **Direct Explanation** – An unfamiliar term may also be introduced in the text with a direct explanation or definition. Again, this is a technique used frequently in textbooks or other forms of technical writing.

   The principle of *inertia* implies that a body in motion tends to remain in motion and a body at rest tends to remain at rest.

   Government is said to exist to settle conflicts and to allocate materials and benefits.

4. **Punctuation** – Here a new term may be followed by a definition or explanation set off by commas, dashes or parentheses. For example, in the following sentence, the specific technical definition of "I" is more clear when this term is explained in parentheses.

   Mead distinguished what he called the "I" (the spontaneous, self-interested, impulsive, unsocialized self)...

   The term "cognitive abilities" in the next sentence is defined by all of the words following the dash:

   The mind is a social product; and, indeed, one of the most important achievements of socialization is the development of *cognitive abilities*— intellectual capacities such as perceiving, remembering, reasoning, calculating, believing.

5. **Synonyms** – A complex term may be followed by a simpler, more commonly understood word that means much the same as the unfamiliar

word. The author is attempting to provide the reader with an explanation/definition, in this instance, by using a comparison.

Too much *cholesterol* causes blood disease by clogging arteries like hard water deposits clog up plumbing pipes.

Insomnia cannot be corrected by sleeping pills; no drug-induced sleep can substitute for a normal sleep.

6. **Antonyms** – You may be able to determine the meaning of an unknown word if you are aware of the sentence structure and understand that the author is presenting a contrast within the sentence. The author is explaining or saying something that is opposite in meaning from the unfamiliar word that needs to be learned.

The young swimmer lacked the *perseverance* of her older team mates who would never quit before the end of the race.

The *socialization* process certainly wasn't working with Henry, as he hardly spoke to anyone at the party.

7. **Inferences** – Sometimes it is necessary to infer the meaning of an unfamiliar word by studying not simply the one sentence, but also those surrounding it. Sometimes meaning must be found through a combination of the author's use of the word and the reader's background and experience. The author often "paints a picture of meaning" rather than concretely defining or explaining the word in the sentence. Study the following examples carefully to see if you can *infer* what is meant.

A youngster often makes his first independent purchase as early as age five. For at least a year prior to this purchase, his parents have been diligently training him in the art of *consumption*. This training includes such activities as retrieving a box of cereal from the supermarket shelf and giving the squeeze test to a loaf of bread. The child soon discovers that many satisfactions can be obtained from purchase behavior. Not only is it a source of such things as sweets and toys, but it is also a way of expressing maturity.

McNeal, J. U., *Consumer Behavior: An Integrative Approach*, (1982). Boston: Little, Brown and Co.

Alcohol (above very low blood levels) is a depressant which *anesthetizes* brain control areas and the central nervous system is put to sleep. In addition, a person can become dependent upon alcohol. A person may become an alcohol addict just as one may become a heroin or nicotine addict.

National Institute on Alcohol Abuse and Alcoholism, *Participant Handbook: A Prevention Program*, (July, 1978). US Dept. of Health, Education and Welfare, Washington, D.C.

ACTIVITY 1 : Context-Clue Discovery Strategies

Following is an excerpt from a technical manual on clinical nursing. Certain words are boxed. *On a sheet of paper write out which context-clue discovery strategy you used to figure out each word. Review the seven strategies:*

1. Definitions
2. Signal Words
3. Direct Explanation
4. Punctuation
5. Synonyms
6. Antonyms
7. Inferences

Reducing Risks for Infection

Planned nursing strategies to reduce the risk of transmission of organisms from one person to another include the use of meticulous medical and surgical asepsis. **Asepsis** is the freedom from infection or infectious material. There are two basic types of asepsis: medical and surgical. **Medical asepsis** includes all practices intended to confine a specific microorganism to a specific area, limiting the number, growth, and spread of microorganisms. **Surgical asepsis** or sterile technique, refers to those practices that keep an area or objects free of all microorganisms; it includes practices that destroy all microorganisms and spores. A **spore** is a round or oval structure enclosed in a tough capsule. Some microorganisms assume this structure in response to adverse conditions; in this form, they are highly resistant to destruction. Sterile technique is required for invasive procedures, such as injections, intravenous therapy, or urinary catheterization.

Maintaining Surgical Asepsis

An object is **sterile** only when it is free of all microorganisms. It is well known that surgical asepsis is practiced in operating rooms, labor and delivery rooms, and special diagnostic areas. Less known, perhaps, is that surgical asepsis is also employed for many procedures in general care areas (i.e., procedures such as administering injections, changing wound dressings, performing urinary catheterizations, and administering intravenous therapy). In these situations, all of the principles of surgical asepsis are applied as in the operating or delivery room; however, not all of the sterile techniques that follow are always required. For example, before an operating room procedure, the nurse generally puts on a mask and cap, performs a surgical hand scrub, and then dons a sterile gown and gloves. In a general care area, the nurse may only perform a hand wash and don sterile gloves.

Hand Washing

Hand washing is important in every setting where people are ill, including hospitals. It is considered one of the most effective infection control measures. The goal of hand washing is to remove **transient microorganisms** that might be transmitted to the nurse, clients, visitors, or other health care personnel.

Any client may harbor microorganisms that are currently harmless to the client yet potentially harmful to another person or to the same client if they find a **portal of entry**. It is important that hands be washed at the following times to prevent the spread of these microorganisms: before eating, after using the bedpan or toilet, and after the hands have come in contact with any body substances, such as sputum or drainage from a wound. In addition, health care workers should wash their hands before and after any direct client contact.

For routine client care, the CDC recommends a **vigorous** hand washing under a stream of water for at least 10 seconds using bar soap, granule soap, soap-filled tissues, or antimicrobial liquid soap (Garner and Favero 1985, p. 7). Liquid soaps are frequently supplied in dispensers at the sink. Antimicrobial soaps are usually provided in high-risk areas, e.g., the newborn nursery. In the following situations, the CDC recommends antimicrobial hand-washing agent, with any chemical germicides listed with the Environmental Protection Agency:

- when there are known multiple resistant bacteria
- before **invasive** procedures
- in special care units, such as nurseries and ICUs

This book recommends that the hands be held down (below the elbows) when they are soiled with body substances and during routine hand washing so that the microorganisms are washed directly into the sink. For surgical asepsis, the hands should be held above the elbows so that the water runs from the cleanest to the least clean area. Nurses usually dry their hands with paper towels, discarding them in an appropriate container immediately after use.

Kozier, B., Erb, G., Blais, K., Johnson, J. Y., and Temple, J. S., *Techniques In Clinical Nursing, 4th Ed.*, (1993). Redwood City, CA: Addison-Wesley, pp. 134-135, 136-137. Used with permission.

Difficult Words

1. asepsis   Definition _____

Context-clue strategy used _____

2. medical asepsis   Definition _____

Context-clue strategy used _____

3. surgical asepsis   Definition _____

Context-clue strategy used _____

4. spore   Definition _____

                      Context-clue strategy used _____

5. sterile   Definition _____

                      Context-clue strategy used _____

6. transient
microorganisms   Definition _____

                      Context-clue strategy used _____

7. portal of entry   Definition _____

                      Context-clue strategy used _____

8. vigorous   Definition _____

                      Context-clue strategy used _____

9. invasive   Definition _____

                      Context-clue strategy used _____

A C T I V I T Y 2 : Using Picture Clues

Sometimes pictures in technical manuals can give you clues to word meanings. Follow the directions for Activity 1, but this time, use the passage and the picture to figure out the difficult word.

Power Brake Vacuum Booster Operation

All vehicles use a 270 mm single diaphragm power brake vacuum booster.

The power brake booster can be identified if required, by the tag attached to the body of the booster assembly (Fig. 1). This tag contains the following information: The production part number of the power booster assembly, the date it was built, and who was the manufacturer of the power brake vacuum booster.

NOTE: The power brake booster assembly is not a

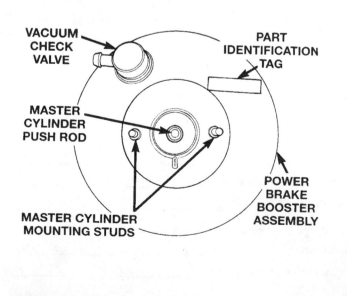

VACUUM CHECK VALVE

PART IDENTIFICATION TAG

MASTER CYLINDER PUSH ROD

POWER BRAKE BOOSTER ASSEMBLY

MASTER CYLINDER MOUNTING STUDS

ponent and must be replaced as a complete assembly if it is found to be faulty in any way. The check valve located in the power brake booster (Fig. 1) is not repairable but it can be replaced as an assembly separate from the power brake booster.

The power brake booster reduces the amount of force required by the driver to obtain the necessary hydraulic pressure to stop vehicle.

The power brake booster is vacuum operated. The vacuum is supplied from the intake manifold on the engine through the power brake booster check valve (Fig. 1) and (Fig. 2).

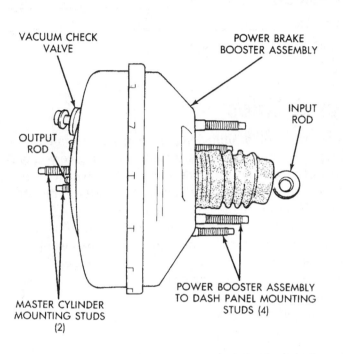

VACUUM CHECK
VALVE

POWER BRAKE
BOOSTER ASSEMBLY

INPUT
ROD

OUTPUT
ROD

MASTER CYLINDER
MOUNTING STUDS
(2)

POWER BOOSTER ASSEMBLY
TO DASH PANEL MOUNTING
STUDS (4)

As the brake pedal is depressed, the power brake boosters input rod moves forward (Fig. 2). This opens and closes valves in the power booster, allowing atmospheric pressure to enter on one side of a diaphragm. Engine vacuum is always present on the other side. This difference in pressure forces the output rod of the power booster (Fig. 2) out against the primary piston of the master cylinder. As the pistons in the master cylinder move forward this creates the hydraulic pressure in the brake system.

The different engine combinations used on this vehicle require that different vacuum hose routings to the power brake vacuum booster be used.

All vacuum hoses must be routed from the engine to the power brake vacuum booster without kinks, excessively tight bends or potential for damage to the vacuum hose.

The power brake vacuum booster assembly mounts on the engine side of the dash panel, and is connected to the brake pedal by the input push rod (Fig. 2). A vacuum line connects the power booster to the intake manifold. The master cylinder is bolted to the front of the power brake vacuum booster assembly.

Chrysler Corporation. *Service Manual: Town & Country, Caravan & Voyager,* (1995). pp. 5-3–5-4. Used with permission.

Difficult Words

1. power brake booster

Definition _____

Context-clue strategy used _____

2. vacuum

Definition _____

Context-clue strategy used _____

3. valves

Definition _____

Context-clue strategy used _____

4. combinations

Definition _____

Context-clue strategy used _____

Using Structural Clues

Language context is a powerful tool for unlocking meanings of unfamiliar words in your reading. However, at times, using the context will give you only a vague idea of the definition. You may still have to expend further time and energy to determine the meaning. Sometimes it may be faster to use the structure of the word to unlock the meaning of an unfamiliar word.

Understanding word structure gives you an additional approach to use when you meet unfamiliar words in your reading. If you know the meaning of a root word and its prefix or suffix you can derive the word's definition. This approach can be very helpful in reading required in the sciences and other technical subjects, for many of the concepts presented in such courses have labels which are derivatives from other languages.

A C T I V I T Y 3 : Practice with Word Structures

Following is a list of meanings of common root words (basic core of a word that carries its meaning) prefixes and suffixes. See Appendix B for additional listings. A prefix is a word element put before the root word to qualify its meaning and a suffix is an element put after the root word to form an entirely new word. Each entry below has one or more examples of root words, prefixes and suffixes. Use the meaning and example given to learn the meaning. Work with your classmates in a small group to generate new words as examples. See if you can generate a new word for each entry.

Common Roots

Root	Meaning	Example
ag, act	to do	enact
aqua	water	aqueous
bene, volo	good, wish	benevolent
dent, dont	tooth	orthodontist

fac, fic, fy	make, do	manufacture
graph	write	graphite
ject, de	throw, from	dejected
manu	hand	manufacture
mov, mot, mob	remove	motivate, remove
phil	love	philosophy

Common Prefixes

a-, an-	not, without, lacking	amoral
amphi-	on both sides, around	amphitheater
centi-	hundred	century
circum-	around	circumstance
contra-, dicto-	against, say, speak	contradiction
dis-	not	dissatisfied
inter	between, among	interact
per-	through, very, thoroughly	perceive
pro-	in favor of, advancing	promote
super-	above, beyond	supercede
tri-	three	triple

Common Suffixes

-able, ible	able	visible
-acy	quality, state, office	piracy
-ance, -ence	adjective- or noun-forming suffix	insurance
-ation, -ition	combination of -ate and -ion used for forming nouns	creation
-ity	used to form nouns expressing state or condition	familiarity
-mony	result or condition, denotes action or condition	testimony
-tude	indicates noun formed from adjective	altitude

A C T I V I T Y 4 : Practice with Roots and Affixes

Use the root words, suffixes and prefixes you have just learned in Activity 3 and your dictionary to determine the meanings of these underlined words.

My uncle was so sick he decided to see a <u>pathologist</u>.

Many people believe that under certain conditions, the human mind can <u>transcend</u> the laws that control the physical world.

One of the best-known types of psychological phenomena is that of pre-cognition.

Psychologists often ask their graduate students to record their introspections during specific activities.

Activity in your sympathetic nervous system prepares you for fighting, for fleeing, and for feeding.

Behaviorists give little credence to biology, believing that the only thing your genes do for you is to program you to your environment.

He acted like an automaton as he routinely went about his daily business.

The most important abolitionists wrote harsh indictments of the slavery system.

Word Attack Plan

You can systematically try to figure out unfamiliar words by using the following word attack plan. You'll use the dictionary less when you use this plan.

Step 1   Use context clues to determine the meaning from how the word is used in the sentence. Use the seven context clue discovery strategies explained previously. Remember that the word must make sense in the sentence.

Step 2   Take off the ending of the word. The word may look "new" because of certain endings such as s, r, d, es, ed, er, est, al, ing.

Step 3   Break the word into syllables. Look for prefixes, suffixes, and root words that are familiar. Don't be worried about breaking the word up two or three ways.

Step 4   Sound the word out. Break the word into syllables and sound each syllable slowly. Do you know a word that begins the same? That ends the same? This will help you sound it out.

Step 5   Check the glossary in the back of the text, if the book has one.

Step 6   Ask a friend in class or the teacher what the word means.

Step 7   As a *last* resort, check the dictionary for the meaning.

Practice using this seven-step plan in your reading to attack unfamiliar words.

Thinking About Words

Become curious about words. Don't be afraid to tackle an unfamiliar or technical word and don't simply skip over it. Learn to think about words and their meanings. Consider the following quote:

> What, then, is a good thinker? And how does he differ from a poor thinker? First, the good thinker is often favored with both an unusually rich and active imagination and an accurate sense of intuition. As mentioned earlier, there is little knowledge available about these abilities. How they work and whether they can be strengthened in a person are matters we can only guess about. They are not subject to any known kind of human control.

V. R. Ruggiero. *Beyond Feelings: A Guide to Critical Thinking,* (1975). Alfred Publishing Co.

Like the quote says, you need to let your "rich and active imagination" soar when thinking about new words. Your hunches about meanings of words (intuition) often will be correct. By *visualizing* words you can remember them better. Visual images are powerful and are likely to help you remember the word when you read it again. You can practice doing the following:

Word	Definition	Visualization
ornate	fancy; decorated	picture of girl in a fancy dress

ACTIVITY 5 : Practice with Visualization

Visualize the following words, then draw a scene that represents each.

Word	Definition
exasperation	extreme irritation; embitterment
simulation	pretending; imitation
glacier	a moving river of ice
intellectual	pursuits of the mind; possessing a high degree of understanding
pemmican	dried, condensed meat

Chunking of Words

As we noted in Chapter 7, words bombard our brains and information is viewed and either discounted or stored in an immediate memory system called **short term memory**. To transfer short term memory into permanent, or **long term memory**, the brain has to perform several functions. First, the brain has to decide whether the information is important. If all information in short term memory were "pushed" over into long term memory, a phenomenon would occur called **information overload**. Therefore, the brain by nature is a selective organ, committing to permanent memory only those items that are absolutely necessary for it to retain. This is why you can remember the phone number of the person you are doing business with until the business is completed. Soon after the number is forgotten. By chunking information together, we can learn information more readily.

If you stop your reading often to review and to categorize information by chunking, you will remember more of what you've read. Notice how the key words from this next passage on homeowners' insurance policies are chunked under categories.

Comprehensive personal liability, a form of casualty insurance, is included in various homeowners and renters policies. This coverage provides protection if you or other members of your household become legally liable for accidental injuries to others or for accidental damage to the property of others. For example, the following would be covered by comprehensive personal liability insurance:

- Injuries you may cause to other individuals while engaging in a sport, such as hunting, playing golf, or playing baseball.

- Injuries sustained by guests, repair-service people, or delivery personnel while on your premises.

- Injuries sustained by a mail carrier who is hurt by your dog.

Conover, H. H., Gordon, S. D. and Ramstetter, V. M. *Business Dynamics*, (1989). Mission Hills, CA: Glencoe Publishing Co., p. 363.

Here is the result of this "chunking" process for the previous passage:

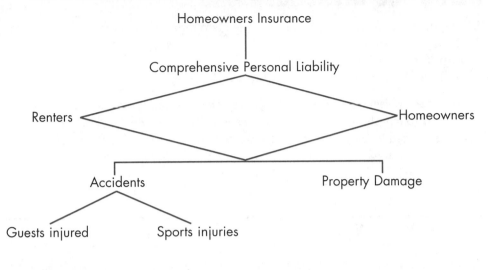

A C T I V I T Y   6 :   Practice Chunking

Following is a passage from a nursing education technical manual on Common Feeding and Nutritional Problems in Infants. *We have* boxed *all the difficult words which are key concepts to be learned in the passage. Individually (or in a small group) try to chunk these terms into a diagram that can be learned more easily for a test.*

Colic refers to paroxysmal intestinal cramps due to the accumulation of excessive gas. It is most common during the first 3 or 4 months of age. The infant may pass gas rectally or belch it up, and experiences great discomfort and pain. He or she cries, becomes red in the face, and draws the arms and legs up to the body. The abdomen feels firm when palpated. One or several factors may cause colic, among them too rapid feeding, overfeeding, excessive intake of carbohydrate, excessive air swallowing, and insufficient burping (bubbling) during feedings.

When intakes of formula are too small (underfeeding), the infant becomes hungry, irritable, underweight, and constipated. The problem can be corrected by increasing the amount and frequency of formula and/or increasing the caloric content of the feedings. When intakes of formula are too large (overfeeding), the infant gains weight faster than the average, regurgitates and may vomit, and has frequent large stools or diarrhea. In this case the formula intake is decreased.

Kozier, B. and Erb, G. *Techniques In Clinical Nursing: A Comprehensive Approach,* (1982). Reading, MA: Addison Wesley Publishing Co.

Using the Dictionary

When you have used all of the approaches explained in this chapter to unlock the meaning of an unfamiliar word and you are still unsure of its meaning, it is appropriate to use the dictionary.

Here is the dictionary entry for the word *dimorphism*:

di - mor - phism\-,fiz- əm\n:[ISV]: the condition or property being dimorphic or dimorphous as a: difference between two individuals that might be expected to be similar or identical; b: crystallization of a chemical compound in two different forms. (*Webster's Seventh New Collegiate Dictionary*)

A C T I V I T Y 7 : Using Your Dictionary

This dictionary entry may be confusing at first, so let's take a closer look at it:

a. What is the purpose of \-,fiz- əm?
b. What does *n* mean?
c. What does [ISV] mean? How could you find this out?
d. Dimorphism means the condition or property of being dimorphic or dimorphous. Is this a helpful definition? Why or why not?
e. Which definition (a. or b.) gives you more information?
f. Where will you look to find more information about this word?

The dictionary should be used when none of the other strategies described in this chapter unlock the meaning of the word. Using the dictionary, however, can be time-consuming as you must have realized when you did Activity 7. Use your dictionary only when other methods of unlocking meaning have not been successful.

The TOAST System of Vocabulary Study

Have you ever had a teacher who gave you lists of words to define using the dictionary and then memorize for a test? As soon as the test was over, did you put the list aside and forget many or most of the words? Some of the words may still be with you, but others you've most likely forgotten. This occurs because you had little to do with creating the list. When you make your own vocabulary list, there is a greater chance that you will remember the meanings of the words. To ensure that new words become a lasting part of your vocabulary, you will need to make a concerted effort to learn and use a systematic approach of study. The following steps will help you enhance and increase your vocabulary.

TOAST (Dana and Rodriguez, 1992) is a vocabulary study system utilizing an acronym to help you learn words in a systematic way. The steps in this vocabulary study technique are as follows:

T	**Test**	Self-test to determine which vocabulary terms you cannot spell, define, or use in sentences.
O	**Organize**	Organize these words into semantically related groups; arrange words into categories by structure or function, such as those that sound alike or are the same part of speech; categorize words as somewhat familiar or completely unfamiliar.
A	**Anchor**	"Anchor" the words in memory by using a key-word method (assigning a picture and caption to a vocabulary term), tape-recording definitions, creating a mnemonic device, or mixing the words on cards and ordering them from difficult to easy.
S	**Say**	Review the words by calling the spellings, definitions, and uses in sentences to another student. The first review session begins 5 to 10 minutes after initial study and is followed at intervals by several more.
T	**Test**	Immediately after each review, self-administer a posttest in which you spell, define, and use in context all the vocabulary terms with which you originally had difficulty. The response mode may be oral, written, or silent thought.

Dana, C. and Rodriquez, M. (1992). "TOAST A System To Study Vocabulary" *Reading Research and Instruction*, 31, 4, pp. 78-84.

A C T I V I T Y   8 :   Using the TOAST System

Read three short passages from textbooks or use the additional readings in the Appendix of this textbook. Use the TOAST method to learn any words that you do not know. Try to find at least one difficult word in each passage. A passage may have more than one word that you have to TOAST.

Ethanol

Although there are several kinds of alcohol, such as methyl (wood) and isopropyl (rubbing) alcohols, ethyl alcohol (or its scientific name, ethanol) is the substance contained in all alcoholic beverages. The ethanol concentration in a beverage indicates the relationship between the volume of total liquid and the amount of alcohol in a drink.

Obviously the concentration of ethanol varies from one kind of drink to another. The ethanol (absolute alcohol) content in American distilled spirits varies from 40 to 50 percent, while table wines range from 10 to 14 percent, and most American beers contain 4 percent.

National Institute on Alcohol Abuse and Alcoholism, *Participant Handbook: A Prevention Program*, (July, 1978). U.S. Dept. of Health, Education, and Welfare, Washington, D.C.

Videodisc

A videodisc is a magnetic disk device that records both the video impulses (pictures) and audio impulses (sound) of a TV signal and is available for instant replay. Videodiscs can store huge quantities of data. For example, one videodisc can store up to 2GB on each side of the disk platter; that is equivalent to approximately 5500 double-density (360KB) floppy disks or 54,000 graphic images. This tremendous storage capability can be interfaced with a computer to become an effective educational training tool for both adults and children. A videodisc player can be connected to a TV monitor and a microcomputer for use in the classroom.

In one example of the use of a computer-videodisc system, a computer's software program controls the presentation of material on the videodisc. For example, once a lesson is started, the computer selects the appropriate textual material to be displayed to the TV monitor as well as movie segments (complete with commentary) or a particular part of the videodisc. After the lesson has been presented, the computer will test the student's understanding of the material by requesting him/her to key-in the answers. If, after grading the test, the computer detects a poor score, it again interfaces with the videodisc player to present a review segment of the lesson. Conversely, if the test score was good, the students' test results are recorded on the microcomputer's floppy disk, and the next lesson is prepared.

Clark, J. F., Allen, W. W. & Klooster, D. H. *Computers and Information Processing: Concepts and Applications, 2nd Ed.*, (1990). Cincinnati, Ohio South-Western Publishing Co., p. 120.

Depreciation for Part of a Year

A plant asset may be disposed of at any time during its useful life. When a plant asset is disposed of, its depreciation from the beginning of the current fiscal year to date of disposal is recorded. For example, adjusting entries for depreciation expense were last recorded on December 31, 1988. The table is discarded on June 30, 1989. Before entries are made for the disposal of the table, six months' depreciation must be recorded. The six months' depreciation is for the period from January 1 to June 30, 1989.

Swanson, R. M., Ross, K. E., and Hanson, R. D. *Century 21 Accounting*, (1988). Cincinnati, Ohio: South-Western Publishing Co., p. 208.

SUMMARY

Words are powerful and important tools for success in life. You can learn and remember new words by practicing the following methods:

1. Use the seven strategies for decoding context clues.
   Definitions
   Signal words
   Direct explanation
   Punctuation
   Synonyms
   Antonyms
   Inferences

2. Use picture clues.

3. Use structural clues, analyzing root words, prefixes and suffixes.

4. Follow a word attack plan.

5. Visualize words.

6. Recite words.

7. Chunk words.

8. Use the dictionary.

9. Use the TOAST system.
   Test
   Organize
   Anchor
   Say
   Test

WRITER'S WORKSHOP

Start a "vocabulary log" for all your classes where you record a definition of the word and use the word in a sentence. You can keep these words on 3" × 5" cards if you wish. Such a card would look like this:

Word _____
Definition_____
Use in sentence found _____
Your use in a new sentence _____

FINAL CHECK

Use the following words to complete this check of what you learned in the chapter.

system	read	dictionary	attack
chunking	visualization	surface	skip
structure	context	reciting	deep

It is important to build a strong vocabulary. Learning new words helps you to _____ with more fluency and comprehend better. Specialized words are particularly difficult because they often have both _____ meaning and _____ meaning. You shouldn't _____ words that you do not know. Rather you should attempt to figure out the meaning through _____ or through the _____ of the word. This chapter has offered several interesting ways to figure out new words, such as a word _____ plan and through _____ techniques. Also ways were explained to get you to retain the meanings of the words, such as _____ meanings and _____ words into hierarchies that show relationships. Also the chapter explained how to use the _____ and to use a special study _____ called TOAST.

The Reading Writing Connection

CHAPTER

9

CHAPTER OBJECTIVES

This chapter will help you to see how closely reading and writing are connected. After completing Chapter Nine, you will be able to:

● understand how audience and purpose affect writing.

● see that using appropriate word choices makes good writing.

● analyze and use voice effectively in writing.

● practice with language.

Chapter Outline

I. Elements of Good Writing

II. Deciding on Appropriate Language

III. Defining Audience and Purpose

IV. Characteristics That Create Voice

V. Increasing Your Readability

VI. Writing That's Reader Friendly

OPENING ACTIVITY

Thomas Jefferson's advice applies to writers and is appreciated by readers. When you are reading to find information and have a specific purpose in mind, you certainly welcome a text that follows this rule. The following activity will demonstrate this clearly. Imagine that some friends sent you the following note:

> *"The most valuable of all talents is that of never using two words when one will do."*
>
> THOMAS JEFFERSON

June 10, 1995

Our Dearest Elizabeth,

It is with expectant hope and sincere devotion that we most cordially invite you to our humble abode for the express purpose of dining and sharing your company with us on the twenty-fourth of June at an hour most convenient to you. We respectfully desire your response for acceptance. We await your answer with great anticipation.

Most sincerely yours,

The Bradleys

If you were able to read through this easily and understand it, congratulations! If you got bored, frustrated or confused trying to get the point or had to go back and read parts of it again—well, join the club.

List some of the problems with this writing. It's supposed to be a friendly invitation. Be specific in your list.

As Thomas Jefferson advised, writing that communicates well must be clear. Look at the revised version of this invitation:

Dear Liz,

We're having a barbecue on Saturday, June 24th at 6pm. Please join us. Call us if you can come.

Hope to see you there,

Bill and Joan

Try writing an invitation to a friend that *is* like the first "Dear Elizabeth" sample. Exchange invitations with a classmate and write a clear and simpler revision. Make words work for you. Don't use two when one will do! Choose exact words that communicate the necessary information.

Elements of Good Writing

As the Opening Activity and your thinking about writing have shown you, there are two key elements readers look for in a piece of good writing:

- clear communication

- a personal connection

Readers want to feel that the writer is speaking directly to them, and they want to feel that the time it takes to read what a writer has written is worth it. These two basic conditions cause readers to invest time in reading. If it seems that the emphasis here is on the readers or audience, you should understand that writing without a reader in mind makes little sense. You should always consider your readers. Consider your reader or audience for each of the following pieces of writing:

- an invitation

- an answer to a question on a test

- a note to a friend

- a procedure for a worker

- a formal letter

- a report to give information

- directions

- a proposal for a project

You decide what to write based on who you think will be reading your writing. Keeping this in mind will determine *what* you write and *how* you write it. Good writing is judged simply by a reader: whether what the writer meant is clear or not!

A C T I V I T Y 1 : A Serious Proposal

Interested students from your school are writing proposals to the school board suggesting how excess funds in the amount of $10,000 should be used. A proposal is simply a paper that offers a suggestion for action, supportive reasons and an expected outcome. The school board will review each proposal and select the one that will benefit the students and school the most. The members of the school board include the following people:

School Board of Education

Ronald Sheldon	– President of Dyna-Graphics—printing company
Lois Weston	– School guidance counselor
Donald Miller	– Accountant for Karston Technologies—computer company
Angela Boyce	– Head librarian for the city public library
Jack Eagler	– Botanist, owner of Greenhurst Nursery
Christine Farber	– Artist, owner of Seraph Studios
Dr. John Ziegler	– Meteorologist for WZAR–TV
Lisa Darrow	– Managing editor for *Around Town*, historical magazine

Choose one of the board members from this list. Write a proposal aimed at persuading this particular board member to consider your proposal. You should appeal to this person directly basing your proposal on what you suspect this board member might favor. Use the profession of the particular person as a hint to guide you in your proposal for what to do with this money.

The purpose of your proposal is to get your particular board member to agree with your suggestion for the $10,000. Your audience is not the entire board but the person you select. Write a proposal to influence and persuade this particular individual.

You can design your proposal to look like the following model:

Dear Mr. or Ms. *(last name)*:

As a student at *(name of school)*, I am proposing that the excess money in the amount of $10,000 be used . . .
>> *(Describe in detail your suggestion.)*

My reasons for this are . . .
>> *(Supply several persuasive reasons.)*

The specific results of using the money for my proposal will be . . .
>> *(Give short term and long term outcomes.)*

Sincerely,

Deciding on Appropriate Language

With a variety of forms of language available, it's important for you to choose the one right for the audience or occasion. Appropriate language is always a writer's choice. Slang, as one form of language, has its place. Often slang is interesting and clear to those who know it, but language that works is always the best type to use. Readers expect a certain type of language based on several factors:

- the topic
- the situation
- the writer/speaker
- the form

A writer who uses the appropriate or "the right" words has a head start with communication. A writer selects words for good reasons. Sometimes the decisions are natural and made quickly.

For example, look at a message left on the kitchen table:

Went for a spin around the block.
Be back at 5. How about pizza for dinner?

>> *Me*

The audience or reader for this note is clear. The language is appropriate, the information is to the point and the question is a nice way of suggesting what you *really want* for dinner. The signature is not confusing or inappropriate, especially if the handwriting is identifiable. This short, information-packed message has a purpose. The informal style works well in this case, and probably the writer didn't spend a lot of time composing this note. We write many notes like this without outlining what we'll say. The *message* or *information* is most important here.

A C T I V I T Y 2 : **The Note's Tale**

*Use the kitchen note, on the previous page, to answer why you **wouldn't** use this type of language or form in the following situations:*

- a report at work
- an essay in history
- a letter to a company
- a reader who you don't know
- a speaker of English as a second language

As a writer, these answers will show how you'll "choose to write." Your answers will help you prepare a **strategy** for writing. All situations call for the right kind of language. You judge if an informal or formal voice is needed. Finding the best words is part of the process.

Defining Audience and Purpose

So, as you have read and practiced, good writers always consider the person or audience they are writing for and the purpose of a piece of writing. In school, you may begin writing when an idea comes to mind. You might have an idea of who the audience is and your purpose for writing, yet these are not often clear enough to guide you in the many writing decisions you'll need to make. Always attempt to determine the following information:

- Who is my audience?
- What am I trying to do with this piece?

The simple note on the kitchen table was written after these two important questions were answered by the writer. In this case, these decisions were made in seconds. The audience was someone familiar—a mother, wife, father or husband—and the purpose was clear—to inform and suggest an idea. The strategy used to create this note is similar in many writing situations—even writing that's longer and more complex. All writers keep their readers in mind.

So, talking about writing without reading is like talking about breathing in, without breathing out. The connection is so important that one without the other makes the transaction incomplete. You've got to do them both!

A C T I V I T Y   3 :   Who and Why?

Try these writing activities. You can also design some of your own that require different language choices.

Write one sentence or several sentences that are appropriate for each audience and that will accomplish the purpose listed. You make up the specifics. Be creative.

Audience	Purpose
Science teacher	To report the results of an experiment
Your employer	To ask for a day off
A group of students	To get them to join a club or activity
A government official	To solve a local problem
A mail carrier	To airmail a package
A friend in the cafeteria	To get her to share her French fries

Share these by reading them aloud. Pay particular attention to the language the writer chose to use.

Characteristics that Create Voice

"Voice is the most important element in writing. It is what attracts, holds and persuades your readers."

DONALD MURRAY

Reading your writing aloud helps you hear the voice in your writing. You hear the sound of your writing played back so you can listen. You can decide if the writing "sounds" the way you want it to or if it needs some fine tuning. Every time you write you are trying out or practicing a new technique or improving your skill in writing in different voices. Concentrate on making the writing sound right! If it doesn't, play with the words.

How do you find your voice? Your voice in writing comes from the type of words you use and the way you put them together in sentences. Like a painter who has favorite subjects or colors or brush strokes, you as a writer have similar identifying marks. You have to look at what you write to spot this.

When a reader wants information, short sentences that contain **specific nouns** like "beagle" instead of "dog" or **specific verbs** like "slammed" instead of "hit" really work best. Readers need specific information. The following items are some of the reasons why readers stop reading:

- illogical pattern
- unfamiliar form
- non-specific word choice
- mechanical errors

You want to avoid letting these elements ruin your writing. If you think that concerning yourself with your patterns, form, word choice, and mechanics is a lot to have to worry about, it is! The good news, though, is that with some attention to these elements your writing will be worth reading.

Recognizing good writing is the first step in your process of producing it. Once you've successfully written a "good" piece, you can use it as a model for future pieces you need to write. If you find a piece of writing that meets these requirements, you can use it as a guide as well.

A C T I V I T Y 4 : What a Voice!

The following sentence lacks a specific voice.

> I am tired.

Convey the idea, meaning or feeling of those three words in the specific voice of each person in the list below. Don't use the word *tired* but write a sentence as the person in the sample might say it. For example, imagine an elderly gold prospector from the old West who might say, **"I need to set myself down and let my weary bones rest up a bit."** Try conveying the feeling of being tired using several of the people from the following list.

College professor	Surfer	Five-year-old	Immigrant
Hockey player	Poet	Sailor	Advertising Agent

Share your one-liners with your classmates. You should be able to hear the different voices of each of these people.

Increasing Your Readability

It is **possible** to make what you write **easier for your reader** to read. Look at some samples of writing that you've done recently. Use these pieces to answer the questions that follow:

- Are most of your sentences about the same length?
- Do many sentences sound the same?
- Does your sentence construction look the same?
- Do many sentences begin or end the same way?
- Do you use the right language for the audience?

Finding your personal answers to any of these questions can help you determine the readability of your writing.

In the field of music there are recognizable forms or types which let listeners categorize different styles. Musicians know a lot about the type of songs they compose. Simply stated: A jazz musician can easily recognize the style of jazz music compared to country-western, classical, rock or rap styles of music. A musician can detect the clues to identify a particular song. Writers and readers can do the same.

For example, a person familiar with technical writing recognizes the format of a technical report and is accustomed to it. This person focuses on the content rather than the unusual style of presentation. In the same way the jazz musician views his music because:

1. it resembles other jazz music styles.
2. it has familiar patterns.
3. it meets expectations.

> *Writing is a question of finding a certain rhythm. I compare it to the rhythms of jazz.*
>
> FRANÇOISE SAGAN

When a reader, in this case a listener, can "place" the piece, then attention to the meaning can be the focus. Writing is no different.

Readers recognize types of writing and can often unconsciously categorize them. When they recognize a poem, a piece of dialogue, a list or a letter, specific expectations or rules immediately apply. For example, when a reader sees something like "Dear Karen," at the beginning of a piece of writing, certain assumptions occur. Based on past experiences with similar styles, a reader predicts what will come next. We play this mind game with all writing we encounter. We make decisions that affect how we'll **make meaning** of the writing.

A C T I V I T Y 5 : Name That Writing!

*Look at the five sample designs on the following page. Each can represent a **type** of writing, a **style** of writing or a particular **piece** of writing. Try naming what each sample looks like to you. Look at our questions to guide you. Share your ideas with your classmates.*

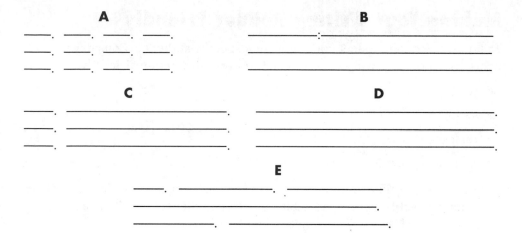

Which design might be a children's story?
Which design might be a business letter?
Which design might be a journal?
Which design might be lyrics of a song?
Which design might be a narrative?
Which design might be a definition?
Which design might be a list?

Writing That's Reader Friendly

If computers are user friendly, why shouldn't writing be reader friendly? If a reader can't understand a piece of writing or it confuses or sends an unintended message, the responsibility to remedy this must fall on the writer. The way a writer adjusts a piece of writing has everything to do with making appropriate choices to adapt it to the reader's experience, knowledge and ability to comprehend.

Imagine writing about using organic pesticides to help promote a safer environment. You might write with the following purposes in mind:

1. to convince farmers to reduce the chemicals they use on their crops.

2. to inform a food company that this is a major consideration for consumers who buy their product.

3. to motivate a legislator to take political action.

Each piece of writing will require different word choices and formats to influence your intended audience. The treatment of a subject changes for different readers, and it should be adjusted to appeal to the readers' sensibilities.

Making Your Writing Reader Friendly

Tailor your writing to meet conditions of a specific audience. Consider your decisions in the following areas to make your writing **reader friendly**:

- word choices
- simplicity
- sentence structure and variety
- presentation or form

Review the three models of writing in the following section. All deal with the same subject but are designed for different audiences. You'll be able to see how these choices affect a piece of writing.

Word Choices

A writer must consciously choose words for an intended reader. Here are three choices:

1. high level, specific, technical words
2. ordinary, middle range words
3. simple, personal, conversational words

Review the following samples to see the difference the three choices of types of words can have on meaning. A chemical engineer familiar with technical terms would understand the statement below with little difficulty:

1. The *methylethylchromide dissipated* proportionately with the increased *molecular excitation* of the *alloy* sample by regulated *electrostatic* impulses.

For a non-engineer or general reader this statement needs word choice adjustments to make it easier to understand.

Consider this next statement which really says the same thing as the first:

2. The *corrosive acid evaporated* more quickly when increased *electrical impulses* were applied to the surface of the *aluminum plate*.

This statement, more in a middle range style, contains words that appeal to a more general audience. You could simplify the statement even further for an audience with little background in this field like this:

3. *The chemical drops* I put on the piece of *metal disappeared quickly* when I turned on the *electricity*.

Choice #3

Does the word choice in the last sample do the best job at communicating the information or message? Although a general reader might think the statement gives sufficient information, it depends on what the reader needs to know. The underlined words are too general for a person in the field who needs very technical information.

Choice #2

The second sample uses more specific word choices and gives more information to a more knowledgeable reader. The word choices provide technical words to give a detailed indication of what occurred in this experiment. The words are less general, yet they are not so technical that only an engineer would understand them.

Choice #1

The first sample has a limited audience. Chemical or electrical engineers would understand the statement. For most people, the level of words selected may prevent rather than promote understanding. The use of "high-tech" language works for a special audience. How "reader friendly" a writer wants to be determines the level of word choices.

In every field—music, business or academic—voice is created by word choices. When clarity and comprehension are primary goals, it's important to select the right words for the right audience.

A C T I V I T Y 6 : Write It Right!

Choose a paragraph from another text. Write the paragraph using high level, middle range or personal language by making different word choices. Identify an audience—a friend, an employer, a teacher, a child—and write the paragraph once again with this reader in mind. Share your original paragraphs and revised ones. Explain your word choices.

Simplicity

Specific nouns connected to specific verbs tend to be easily understood by all readers. For example, a statement that does not employ these simple guidelines might sound like this:

Things happen.

To be more specific, a revised sentence might sound like this:

Hurricanes destroy.

While neither of these sentences fully allows the reader to understand details of meaning, you can see how the second example gives more specific information to the reader. The words selected are concrete and specific. The writer of the second statement is closer to communicating a meaning by using more specific word choices. The style is simple and direct. A reader has a good idea of the topic.

A Variety of Sentence Patterns

Read the following sample paragraph:

Long sentences can increase the difficulty of understanding by general readers making it a chore to read through or follow for any length of time. Technical information, operating directions or exact procedures generally are shorter in length so that readers can easily go step by step through a series of them without confusion. Patterns that are repeated in a piece of writing become familiar to a reader, and if you're like most of us, you probably don't write like this naturally, so you'll have to make an effort to check this in your writing. If you need to use long sentences you should consider the use of a short sentence either at the beginning or end of a block of writing or a paragraph. Short sentences emphasize a point.

A C T I V I T Y 7 : This is Who I Am!

If you analyze the last five sentence paragraph and count the number of words in each sentence you can visually see how the paragraph was constructed.

Total of five sentences in the paragraph:

Sentence 1	–	25 words
Sentence 2	–	28 words
Sentence 3	–	41 words
Sentence 4	–	30 words
Sentence 5	–	5 words

Apply the same procedure to the following **seven sentence paragraph**. Chart the number of words in each of the sentences in the paragraph.

As a writer, be careful to consider the length of your sentences. It's important to use a variety, too. Long sentences aren't always the most effective way to communicate. Don't think that a lot of short sentences are desirable either. The reader can have an impression that you lack sophistication or feel that your ideas don't flow well. Using a variety of sentence lengths makes your writing most interesting. Try it.

Do you see the effect that varying sentence lengths has on a reader? Check your writing for this. Find your own pattern and make some decisions about how you'd like your writing to look and sound. It's a simple and sure-fire way to improve your writing, to make it more "readable."

S U M M A R Y

There is a strong connection between reading and writing. The connection can be simplified by the following chart:

WRITE TO GET READY ———→ READ ———→ WRITE ABOUT
FOR READING   READING

Good writing practice enhances any reading you will do. The elements of good writing are clear communication and a personal connection for the reader. Effective writing keeps the reader in mind. As you write for your audience you must:

- decide on appropriate language.

- define your audience and purpose.

- use an appropriate voice.

- use recognizable forms, types, and styles.

- use language that's reader friendly.

WRITER'S WORKSHOP 1

Choose any two paragraphs from this book or a textbook you are using for a class. Count the sentences and the number of words in each sentence as you did in Activity 7. Look at the pattern of the sentences in the paragraph. Compare what you find. Write your reactions, comments and evaluation. Share these with your classmates.

This technique gives you a good picture of what you're writing or reading. It's called the **Paragraph**, **Sentence**, **Word Technique** or the "**PSW Technique**." The PSW Technique shows you definite patterns. Do you detect specific patterns in certain types of writing? For example, does the pattern of a manual of directions look the same as the pattern for a business letter?

WRITER'S WORKSHOP 2

Read the following selections from a Century 21 Accounting textbook. Apply the PSW Technique to these passages. Passage 1 is entitled "Accounting Principles" and Passage 2 is entitled "Employee Earnings."

Passage 1

ACCOUNTING PRINCIPLES

Anything of value that is owned is called an asset. An amount owned by a business is called a liability. Financial rights to the assets of a business are called equities. The value of the owner's equity is called capital. In a corporation the value of the owner's equity is referred to as stockholder's equity.

An equation showing the relationships among assets, liabilities, and capital is called an accounting equation. The accounting equation may be stated a assets = equities. More commonly the equation is stated as assets = liabilities + capital. The accounting equation is shown in the following T account.

Accounting Equation

(LEFT side)		(RIGHT side)
Assets	=	Liabilities
		+ Capital

The equation is often viewed as forming a "T." Assets are listed on the left side of the T and equities (liabilities and capital) on the right side of the T. Total assets must always equal total liabilities plus capital.

Swanson, R. M., Ross, K. E., and Hanson, R. D. *Century 21 Accounting, 4th Ed.,* (1988). Cincinnati, Ohio: South-Western, p. 19.

Paragraph 1   # of Sentences _____
                     # of Words in each Sentence _____ _____ _____ _____
                                        _____

Paragraph 2   # of Sentences _____
                     # of Words in each Sentence _____ _____ _____ _____

Paragraph 3   # of Sentences _____
                     # of Words in each Sentence _____ _____ _____

Passage 2

EMPLOYEE EARNINGS

An employee's pay rate is usually stated as a rate per hour, day, week, month, or year. Pay is sometimes based on pieces produced per unit of time, such as number of pieces produced per hour.

Supergolf has a biweekly pay period of 80 hours. The basic salary may be supplemented by other types of earnings. For example, in addition to a basic biweekly salary, an employee may receive commissions, cost-of-living adjustments, a share of profits, or a bonus.

Supergolf has three types of employee earnings. First, an hourly salary is paid biweekly to salesclerks and accounting department employees. Second, a biweekly salary is paid to each of the two department supervisors and the store manager. Third, a monthly commission is also paid to each of the department supervisors.

Swanson, R. M., Ross K. E., and Hanson, R. D. *Century 21 Accounting, 4th Ed.,* (1988). Cincinnati, Ohio: South-Western, p. 56.

Paragraph 1   # of Sentences _____
                     # of Words in each Sentence _____ _____

Paragraph 2   # of Sentences _____
                     # of Words in each Sentence _____ _____ _____

Paragraph 3   # of Sentences _____
                     # of Words in each Sentence _____ _____ _____ _____

Look at the patterns of these paragraphs in both of these passages. Write your reactions, comments and evaluations. Compare what you find in these passages to your own writing, your class textbook or this book. Share what you find in a group and with your class.

WRITER'S WORKSHOP 3

Using straight lines and punctuation marks only, draw some of the shapes or designs of the writing you've been working with in school. Share these in class to see if only the outlines of pieces of writing show something. Apply this to several different types of writing and see if classmates can identify the subject, purpose or audience of these pieces of writing. Compare and discuss your findings.

WRITER'S WORKSHOP 4

Find familiar samples of writing to bring into class and share—newspaper articles, famous speeches, short stories, magazine articles, directions for products, etc. Apply the PSW Technique to these. Consider the purpose and audience for each piece. Write your results and thoughts on these to share in class. For example, compare a children's story by Dr. Seuss to the famous government document, *The Declaration of Independence*. What do you see?

FINAL CHECK

See if you can answer these questions after reading this chapter:

1. Reading and writing
   a. are not really closely related.
   b. use exactly the same mental processes.
   c. show ways to communicate knowledge.
   d. have a strong connection.

2. A good reader and writer will
   a. probably not benefit from this book.
   b. practice both language skills together.
   c. have difficulty speaking.
   d. practice these language skills separately.

3. To make your writing more reader friendly, you can
   a. write more neatly.
   b. select appropriate words for audience and purpose.
   c. use slang.
   d. write long sentences which contain a lot of information.

Answers: 1. d.; 2. b.; 3. b.

Appendices

Appendix A

Additional Practice Readings

Painting Tips

PAINTING TIPS

- If you are often bothered by the paint brush being in the wrong place when you are painting, use a magnet on the side of your paint can (Fig. 1). This keeps the brush within easy reach at all times.
- A magnet attaches to the metal can easily and provides an anchor for the metal flange on the paint brush. The brush can be stuck to the magnet or pulled away at any time.
- You will probably find a magnet holder much more convenient than laying the brush across the top of the can. A brush laid across the can often gets paint on the handle and then onto your hands.
- Place a small amount of paint in the middle of a paper plate. Place the paint can in the paint. The plate will stick to the can and catch any drippings from the brush.
- Paint always seems to build up in the lid groove on the can during every painting job. This often causes paint to run down the side of the can.
- You can eliminate this problem by punching several holes in the lid groove with a 4 or 6 penny nail (Fig. 2). These holes permit the paint to drain back into the can each time it accumulates in the lid groove.
- These holes in no way affect the resealing of the can, since the lid seals by pressure on the sides of the groove rather than on the bottom.
- Put any leftover paint in a quart can and seal it tightly—use the regular lid for the can if it is available.
- If the regular lid gets bent or lost, use the plastic lid from a coffee can, which fits smoothly onto the top of many quart cans of paint (Fig. 3).
- The plastic lid makes an airtight seal to keep the paint in good condition until you use it later. You'll also be able to see the color of the paint.

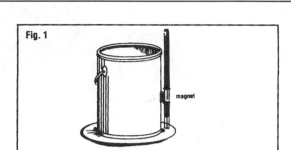

Fig. 1

Use a small magnet to hold your brush to the paint can.

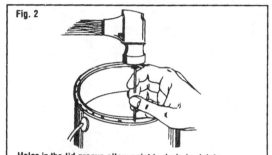

Fig. 2

Holes in the lid groove allow paint to drain back into the can.

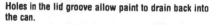
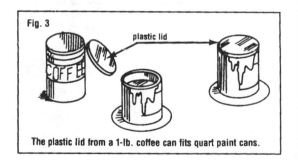

Fig. 3

The plastic lid from a 1-lb. coffee can fits quart paint cans.

- For small touch-up paint jobs, try using a pipe stem cleaner (Fig. 4). A pipe stem cleaner is ideal for applying small quantities of paint on flat or uneven surfaces.
- A pipe stem cleaner is especially handy for reaching into hidden corners and grooves on irregular surfaces.
- Simply discard the pipe stem cleaner when the job is through. There is no clean-up!

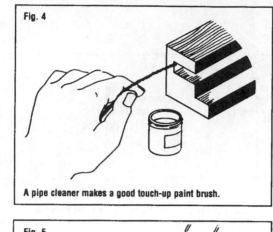

Fig. 4

A pipe cleaner makes a good touch-up paint brush.

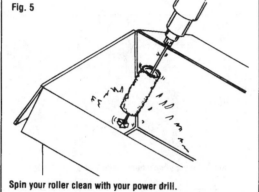

Fig. 5

Spin your roller clean with your power drill.

- Your 1/4" power drill makes an ideal tool for cleaning paint rollers when your painting job is done.
- Remove the roller and pad from the roller handle and attach it to a paint stirrer that fits into the chuck of your drill (Fig. 5).
- For water-base paint, you can dip the roller into clean water and then spin it dry with the drill.
- Use a discarded cardboard box or a newspaper-lined waste can to catch the paint as it is thrown from the roller pad by the spinning drill.

"Tips for Making Home Repairs," HQ® pamphlet. Reprinted courtesy of National Retail Hardware Association.

Installing Paneling

Paneling is one of the easiest things you can do to change the look of a room. The 4 ft. × 8 ft. sheets come in many materials, textures and colors — you may find that choosing the paneling is the toughest part of the job! Your retailer will be happy to help you.

1. ESTIMATE YOUR NEEDS

- To figure how much paneling you'll need, measure in feet the total width of the walls you're covering, then divide by four. This will give you the number of 4 ft. × 8 ft. sheets required. Deduct half a panel for each door, and a quarter panel for each window.

2. INSTALLING ON SOLID BACKING

- First, locate the wall studs. Repair the old wall, ensuring that it is nailed tightly to its framing. The framing behind walls usually runs vertically on 16-inch centers or some-times 24-inch centers. When you find one stud, you can usually locate the others easily by measuring. Or you can use a stud-finder. Either way, mark the locations by snapping or drawing vertical lines along the studs. Then continue the lines (or use tape) several inches out onto both the ceiling and the floor as guides for when the panels cover the marks at the studs.
- Remove all the trim. Take down all moldings in the room: ceiling, floor, and around all open-ings. Take off the electrical receptacle and light switch covers, after you turn off the elec-tricity to them. (Use a neon test light to be sure it's off.) If the ceiling is to be paneled, too, remove all light fixtures by first turning off the electricity and disconnecting them from their wiring. For safety, reinstall the wire nuts or put tape around the exposed wires inside the junction box.

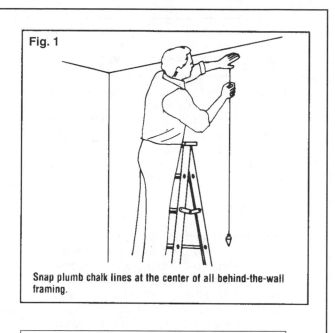

Fig. 1

Snap plumb chalk lines at the center of all behind-the-wall framing.

3. MEASURING AND CUTTING THE PANELS

- Begin putting up the panels in the first corner you see as you enter the room. Trim each panel to 1/4 inch shorter than the ceiling height.
- Get the first corner panel exactly plumb, using a level or chalked plumb line snapped onto the wall (Fig. 1). Its outer edge *must* be centered on a framing member. The edge against the corner may have to be trimmed to bring the outer edge over a stud or furring strip. Double check all your measurements before sawing the panel. Cut with a fine-tooth saw—never use one with coarse teeth. Do the sawing with a table or hand crosscut saw (not rip), working from the *finished* side of the panel (Fig. 2). With a saber saw, cir-cular saw, or radial-arm saw, work from the *back side*.

"Installing Paneling," HQ® pamphlet. Reprinted courtesy of National Retail Hardware Association.

Fence Styles

SELECTING THE FENCE STYLE

There are literally hundreds of variations in fence styles and construction materials.

- Fences like the type shown in Fig. 10 are used primarily for barriers. They are easy to build and provide an adequate barrier. However, they are usually not very decorative and they provide very little, if any, privacy.
- Fences like those illustrated in Fig. 11 provide barriers and are more attractive than an ordinary fence.
- Fences such as those illustrated in Fig. 12 are primarily privacy screens. They can be built as tall as needed out of many different materials. Their primarily purpose is privacy.
- Regardless of the type of fence you plan to build, be sure you know exactly where your property line is located. If you are uncertain about the location of the line, check into it or work out an agreement on the fence location with your neighbor.
- Also, check any local ordinances applying to fences before beginning construction. Call the building department of your local city hall or ask for the local government office that regulates construction to be sure you abide by city codes.
- Fig. 13 illustrates four basic styles of easy-to-build fence. Each style has the same basic top, center and bottom rail construction. However, the fences look entirely different with the various rail treatments.

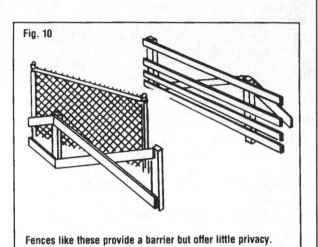

Fig. 10

Fences like these provide a barrier but offer little privacy.

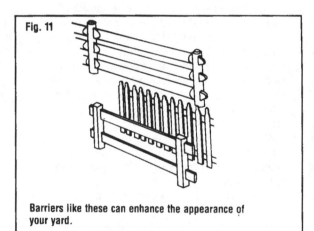

Fig. 11

Barriers like these can enhance the appearance of your yard.

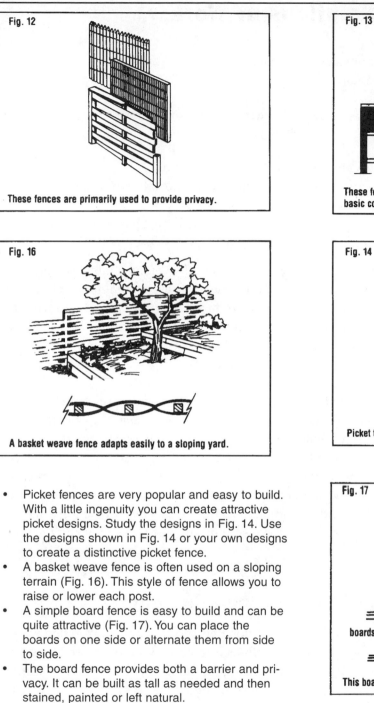

Fig. 12

These fences are primarily used to provide privacy.

Fig. 13

These four easy-to-build styles of fence have the same basic construction.

Fig. 16

A basket weave fence adapts easily to a sloping yard.

Fig. 14

Picket fences can be styled in many ways.

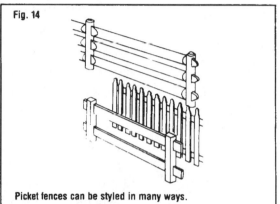

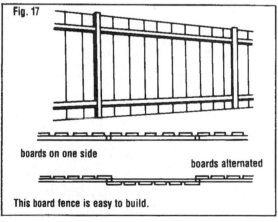

- Picket fences are very popular and easy to build. With a little ingenuity you can create attractive picket designs. Study the designs in Fig. 14. Use the designs shown in Fig. 14 or your own designs to create a distinctive picket fence.
- A basket weave fence is often used on a sloping terrain (Fig. 16). This style of fence allows you to raise or lower each post.
- A simple board fence is easy to build and can be quite attractive (Fig. 17). You can place the boards on one side or alternate them from side to side.
- The board fence provides both a barrier and privacy. It can be built as tall as needed and then stained, painted or left natural.

Fig. 17

boards on one side

boards alternated

This board fence is easy to build.

"Building Wood Fences," HQ® pamphlet. Reprinted courtesy of National Retail Hardware Association.

Human Relations at Work

Objectives

After reading this chapter, you should be able to:
- Explain the importance of good human relations to success on the job.
- Discuss ways to get along with co-workers.
- Identify three reasons why customers patronize a particular business.
- Discuss ways to participate effectively in a task group.

You deal with people every day of your life. You may talk, joke, plan, study, argue, and so on. Some of these dealings are more important than others. For instance, you go into a store to buy a quart of milk. Chances are that your conversation with the clerk won't influence life much. On the other hand, a talk with your boss, co-workers, or teacher just might. Your dealings with others influence your happiness and success. They also may affect others. Ask Kevin.

Guy was supposed to pick up his friend Kevin on the way to school. Guy got up late, and in his hurry to get to school, forgot Kevin. So an unhappy Kevin had to walk two miles to school. He got to school late, missed a test, and had to go to detention after school. Guy's mistake caused problems for Kevin.

Some human relations are pleasant. Others are very difficult. Unless we become hermits, we can't get away from other people. So we need to learn to deal with many kinds of situations. This is especially true for workers. It's true that most fired workers lose their jobs because they can't get along with others.

Bosses, Co-Workers, and Customers

Suppose you and another student don't get along very well. You find yourselves in the same English class. Chances are that you won't need to work closely with the other student. On the job, though, you may have to work closely all week with someone you really don't like. In such cases, you will both need to put personal feelings aside.

At work we have to deal with all kinds of people. These include bosses, co-workers, and customers. We may like some of these people more than others. Even so, we must try to get along with everyone. Understanding our bosses, co-workers, and customers can make this task easier.

Getting Along with Bosses

Most employees have a boss. The boss may be the company's owner, a crew chief, or a department head. Whoever your boss is, you will need to form a working relationship with him or her (reviewed in Chapters 6 and 7).

Good employees try to understand the boss' position. Being a boss is never easy. How would you feel if you had to fire someone, for instance? Bosses sometimes must do this. They must always provide workers with instructions and helpful criticism. Good bosses act in the interest of the company. They don't act out of friendship. Sometimes, workers and bosses do become friends. Even so, this should not influence their work behavior. The company should still come first. If you and your boss aren't friends, that's fine. You can still have a good relationship. (Some bosses make it a policy not to be friends with people they supervise.)

Getting Along With Co-Workers

Strong friendships depend on interpersonal attraction. Think about it. Why do people become your friends? Well, they are probably somewhat like you. We enjoy being with people who are like us in at least some ways. We choose such people for friends, and they choose us. At work, though, interpersonal attraction isn't as important. What is important is doing your share of the work and following rules.

As a new worker, you can be sure that your co-workers will be watching you. They will expect you to do your share of the work. Your co-workers probably won't mind helping you out from time to time. They will expect you to do the same when they need help. But your co-workers won't put up with doing their work and yours, too. At least, they won't for long.

Following the rules is important. Rules make sure that employees in similar jobs receive equal treatment. If you ignore the rules, you are indicating that you are different or better than the other workers. Your co-workers won't like your ignoring the same rules that they are expected to follow.

Sometimes, being different has its place at work. Two examples involve seniority and territorial rights. Seniority refers to the length of time someone has worked for a company. Workers with the most seniority have the most privileges. Respecting seniority rules will help you get along with co-workers.

In January, Tina requested to take a week's vacation during the first week in June. Mrs. Soria, the boss, came to talk to her. It turned out that Sven, who had the same job title as Tina, wanted the same week off. Mrs. Soria told Tina that she couldn't do without both of them that week. Since Sven had been there two years longer than Tina, he would get to take that week. Tina thanked Mrs. Soria for telling her. She then started to think about choosing some other week.

In a work setting, certain unwritten rules about territorial rights may develop. Some workers come to feel that they control a certain office, area, or sales territory. When you are on their turf, they expect you to behave as they wish. An example might be that you are not to bring food into a certain person's office. Or, maybe you aren't supposed to use someone's tools without asking permission first. Be alert for such things. Try to respect other's territorial rights.

Doing your share of the work and following the rules lead to good feelings among co-workers. Other ways to maintain good relationships with co-workers include the following:

- Appearance. Maintain good personal hygiene and grooming. Don't underdress or overdress.

- Courtesy. Be pleasant, friendly, and courteous. Don't force relationships with co-workers. In time, some may become your friends.

- Attitude. Be positive. Don't complain about your job. Clint sometimes gets tired of being a "go-fer" for everyone in the shop. He doesn't let it discourage him, though. Clint is glad to have a job, and looks forward to a promotion soon.

- Interest. Show interest in the job. Pay attention to what co-workers are doing and show them that you feel their interests are important.

- Loyalty. Don't criticize the company or gossip about bosses or co-workers. Those you talk to will wonder what you are saying about them!

- Tolerance. Try to tolerate the opinions, habits, and behaviors of co-workers. Being different is all right. Martha, for instance, is a vegetarian. She eats bean, cucumber and alfalfa sandwiches for lunch. Through her, some co-workers have learned more about good eating habits.

Bailey, Larry. *Working Skills for a New Age,* (1990). Albany, NY: Delmar Publishers.

Components for Profit

Both retailers and vendors are expected to contribute to the profitability of the companies they represent. To contribute profits to their respective organizations while working together effectively, a thorough knowledge and working application of the components for profitable merchandising are necessary. Business judgments depend on the computation and interpretation of figure facts.

The means to improve profits for retailers and vendors alike are accomplished by following the ideas presented throughout this text while keeping in mind the interaction of the basic profit components and the effect decisions will have on generating profits.

Five basic profit components interact to contribute to the profit produced within any retail operation. These five factors are brought together by the retailer's pricing decisions with the results reflected on the income statement.

NET SALES VOLUME

Net sales volume is the total amount of dollars received from the sale of merchandise, less customer returns and allowances, sales taxes, and the retailer's excise taxes collected directly from customers for a specific period of time.

COST OF GOODS SOLD

Cost of goods sold is the total merchandise costs for a specific period of time, including the billed invoice amounts of merchandise purchased, transportation charges incurred, and the costs of preparing merchandise for sale.

GROSS MARGIN OF PROFIT

Gross margin of profit (GM/GP) is the dollar amount remaining after the cost of goods sold is subtracted from the net sales volume. This amount must be high enough to cover the costs of doing business to produce the desired profit.

TOTAL OPERATING EXPENSES

Total operating expenses are the costs incurred in operating the store, not including merchandise expense.

NET OPERATING PROFIT

Net operating profit is profit before other income, other expenses, and income taxes are considered. This is the difference between income and total operating expenses realized from the buying and selling of merchandise. If income exceeds expenses, net operating profit results (otherwise referred to as being "in the black"). Conversely, if total operating expenses are greater than income, the result is net operating loss (also known as being "in the red").

These five basic profit components are formatted on the income statement so that the results are easily comparable to planned sales and expense goals, last year's results, and comparable retail operations for analysis.

These components are represented not only as dollar figures but also as percentages of net sales. Since net sales is valued at 100%, each component is a percent of that and provides the basis for calculating profit contribution in financial accounting. These ratios (quantitative relationships) are used to analyze the financial condition of a company, past to the present. Such ratios are published for most industries to offer comparisons to others in specific business fields. Dun & Bradstreet's Key Business Ratios report, the National Retail Merchants Association Merchandising and Operating Results publication, and industry trade associations provide this information annually.

Paidar, Meridith. The Meridith Group, (1994). *Merchandising Mathematics.* Albany, NY: Delmar Publishers, Inc. pp. 47–48.

Forests in America Today

How Much Is There?

In America today, there are about 738 million acres of forestland. That is about 70 percent as much forestland as when Leif Ericson—and later Christopher Columbus—landed on this continent.

Roughly one-third of that total is referred to as noncommercial forestland. This area of about 250 million acres is made up of land which is generally not suitable for economical tree production. Included in this are swamps, very rough mountainous land, and other areas where trees grow but cannot be economically harvested. Also included are parks, wilderness preservation areas, game refuges, and other areas where timber harvesting is not allowed.

The other two-thirds, about 488 million acres, is generally referred to as commercial forest. But that name is very misleading. The term *commercial forest* simply means that the land is capable of producing economically useful forest. It does not mean that the land is actually being used that way. Almost one-half of this area is not actually available for forest production. Much of it is in small parcels: near homes or in suburban areas, or along highways, streams, or lakes. Still more of this so-called commercial forest is simply not being managed for wood production.

That leaves only about 250 million acres of actual commercial forestland. That makes about one acre of commercially producing forestland for each man, woman, and child in the United States. But, just as the available farmland is being taken over for urban and industrial expansion, so is our forestland. About 12 million acres of United States forestland were converted from growing timber to other uses during a recent seven-year period.

Who owns this forestland? Where is it located? Many people believe that the large timber companies own most of the forest, but, while these large companies do own vast areas of forest, that reputation is not totally deserved.

Of the 488 million commercial forest acres, private individuals (some 4 million of them) own 58 percent, or 283 million acres. Much of the land classified as commercial but not being used for wood production falls into this category.

The next largest holder of forestland is government. Federal, state, and local governments own about 137 million acres (or about 28 percent) of the commercial forest. As before, much of this is not being managed for forest production.

The forest products industries—Weyerhauser, Kraft, Union-Camp, and other corporations—hold about 68 million acres. That represents only about 14 percent of the total, but over 27 percent of the actual producing commercial forestland.

Every state has at least some forestland. To see how much forestland is in your state, see Table 16-1.

While the figures in 16-1 represent total forested area, there are at least some truly commercial forestlands in all 50 states. In fact there are 37,000 certified tree farms in this country. Together, they encompass about 80 million acres of forestland. The typical tree farm is a single family operation of less than 200 acres in size; clearly, on most of these, timber production is not the primary enterprise or source of farm income.

Tree farmers manage their forestland to produce timber, but this often also means better wildlife habitat as well as soil and water management. If you own ten or more acres of forestland, you may be interested in establishing a certified tree farm. If so, contact

The American Tree Farm System
American Forest Institute
1619 Massachusetts Avenue N.W.
Washington, D.C. 20036

Camp, William G. and Thomas B. Daugherty. *Managing Our Natural Resources, 2nd ed.* (1991). Albany, NY: Delmar Publishers.

Use and Reuse of Water

What is the quality of water we use? Most commonly the water we use for washing our clothes, cooking, and bathing is the same quality we use for drinking purposes. If water becomes extremely short in supply, it would be wise to reuse or even reclassify the water we use. Why use excellent quality drinking water to flush our toilets, wash our cars, and water our lawns? We could reserve the top-quality water for drinking purposes or for cooking.

One proposal, which would not be popular, is to recycle all water, even sewage water. Although the suggestion seems repulsive at first, many towns and cities are already doing just that. Consider a series of towns and cities located along a common waterway. The first town draws its water from an upstream source and releases its waste effluents downstream. The next town downstream draws its water from an upstream source, which contains the sewage from the first town. This procedure may continue for hundreds of miles and involve many towns. Each town is recycling water from another town. The main problem facing experts in recycling is the removal of odor, tastes, and salts from the water. Also, if pathogens have entered the water, disease such as infectious hepatitis could become a problem. Nobody wants to think of drinking sewage water, but many people do just that every day.

As stated in another chapter, industry is a large user of water, and has the most to lose if it is not conserved. The federal government is placing tighter pollution standards on industrial water supplies. It is forcing industry to develop ways to use water over and over.

Camp, William G. and Thomas B. Daugherty. *Managing Our Natural Resources, 2nd ed.* (1991). Albany, NY: Delmar Publishers.

Pesticides

A **pesticide** is any substance used to kill organisms unwanted by humans. These include insecticides (insects), herbicides (higher plants), algicides (algae), fungicides (fungi), bactericides (bacteria), nematicides (nematodes), **avicides** (birds), molluscacides (slugs and snails), viruscides (virus), and **rodenticides** (rodents). A more general term for chemicals that are used to kill organisms is biocide.

Nebel described as "first generation" pesticides those early pesticides which were based on inorganic sources, such as sulfur, and compounds of heavy metals such as mercury, lead, and arsenic. Other early insecticides that could also be considered first generation include a number of naturally occurring toxic substances such as salt and petroleum. These were the only pesticides available in large quantity until the 1930's.

Second generation pesticides began to be developed in the 1800's in the form of synthetic organic compounds. The first important second generation pesticide was dichlorodiphenyltrichloroethane (DDT). It was first synthesized in the 1880's, but it was not until 1938 that DDT became recognized as a potentially important insecticide.

DDT was extremely toxic to insects, yet seemed to have no effect on larger animals such as birds, mammals, and humans. It was cheap to manufacture, selling for as little as twenty cents per pound at retail. It could be produced in huge quantities, and was simple to transport and apply. It was so effective that crop production in treated fields increased dramatically. Mosquitoes, the carrier of tropical diseases such as malaria, could be effectively controlled for the first time in history. It appeared that a solution to one of humanity's oldest scourges, insects, might be at hand. The remarkable properties of DDT and the other second generation pesticides that have followed have had massive effects on the human condition and on the environment.

Camp, William G. and Roy L. Donahue. *Environmental Science for Agriculture and the Life Sciences,* (1994). Albany, NY: Delmar Publishers.

Climatic Change

The amount of solar energy reaching the Earth's atmosphere has been fairly constant over the past several million years. But no one knows how much, or even if it has varied over geological time beyond 100 million years. It is certain, however, that the Earth's atmospheric and surface temperatures have varied greatly over time.

The Earth's orbit around the sun is not perfectly stable. Even if it were, the alignment of the planet's axis wobbles slightly. Thus, the climate within a given area may vary enormously across the centuries. As discussed later in Chapter 20, global temperature change has been observed throughout Earth's history, and is not uncommon.

Changing climates drastically affect the biotic components of ecosystems. A shift of only a few degrees can completely change the dominant forms of plant life in an area. During the great ice ages for instance, as the temperatures of the planet's surface cooled, the size and thickness of the ice packs increased. As a result of the transformation of surface water to ice, levels of the Earth's oceans fell by as much as 110 yards below current levels. The ice cover moved across much of Europe, Asia, and North America.

The result was a complete change in the locations of the great biomes in regions that are now North America, Europe, and Asia. What had been tundra was covered by glacial ice. What had been coniferous forest became tundra. What had been temperate regions covered by deciduous forest became coniferous forests, and so on. Recent discoveries indicate that there may have been many ice ages in the Earth's history. Each successive ice age meant massive changes in the biosphere.

But, the ice ages are only one example of this constancy of change. The eruption of Mount Pinatubo in the Philippines during 1991 forced so much volcanic dust into the atmosphere that the albedo of the entire Earth's atmosphere was changed and predicted to remain altered for several years. You may recall from Chapter 1 that the amount of solar energy available for plants to convert to food energy by photosynthesis is controlled in large measure by the reflectivity of the atmosphere. Dust in the atmosphere, like cloud cover, reduces that level of available energy significantly.

Every such environmental change means countless and unforeseeable shifts in the pattern of plants and animals that will dominate and survive within a given ecosystem.

Camp, William G. and Roy L. Donahue. *Environmental Science for Agriculture and the Life Sciences,* (1994). Albany, NY: Delmar Publishers.

The Greenhouse Effect

The **greenhouse effect** is the absorption of solar energy by gases and particulates in the atmosphere. When the energy is absorbed, much of it is expressed as heat. Thus, the greenhouse effect produces a warming of the atmosphere by absorption of solar energy.

As we have seen, not all of the energy reaching the planet is absorbed. Based on the varying albedos of the atmosphere, clouds, atmospheric dust, and differing planetary surfaces, the Earth reflects thirty-five to thirty-seven percent of the solar energy reaching the upper atmosphere. Much of the energy that is not reflected is subsequently radiated into space as long-wave radiant emissions. Much of the rest is captured in chemical reactions in various forms of organic and inorganic compounds. Part of the energy retained by the planet appears to us as latent and perceptible heat.

The energy that is not returned to space as reflected or emitted energy, is absorbed by various surfaces. That part of the energy that is absorbed by the atmosphere produces the greenhouse effect (see Figure 20-6).

Given the amount of solar energy reaching the Earth, climatologists estimate that the planetary mean temperature should be about -0.4° F (about -18° C). In the absence of the greenhouse effect, that is what it most likely would be. But, as we have seen, the current mean global temperature is actually closer to +59° F (+15° C). The difference of about 59.4° F or 33° C has made life on Earth possible ((Lorius, Jougel, Raynaud, Hansen, & LeTreut, 1990).

In an Earth without the greenhouse effect, there would be little free water. Instead of oceans, the world would be covered by massive bodies of ice, with the possible exception of the tropical regions receiving most direct sunlight where small amounts of liquid water might accumulate during the warmest summer days, only to freeze again at night.

Camp, William G. and Roy L. Donahue. *Environmental Science for Agriculture and the Life Sciences,* (1994). Albany, NY: Delmar Publishers.

The Digital Revolution

Computer technology is changing the way we live and work. Digital bits—0s and 1s—are the language of computers, and more and more of the world's information is being converted into digital bits. (The word "bit" comes from two words: b[inary] [dig]it.) Digital CDs have replaced vinyl records. Telephone, radio, and television signals are becoming digital. So are movies, books, photographs, and even paintings.

When desktop personal computers (PCs) were first introduced, they were typically used by individuals who were working on their own projects. As the number of PCs within a workplace increased, they were linked together, forming networks. People working on the same task could communicate with one another, sharing files and information.

Local Area Networks (LANs) have become very common. They have made it possible for workers within one building or location to communicate with one another by computer. Networks allow you to share computer files and databases, to use electronic bulletin boards, and to send and receive electronic mail (e-mail).

Wide Area Networks (WANs), which have similar features to LANs, make it possible to communicate over much greater distances. Today, with the appropriate network telecommunications hardware and software, a person can use a computer to communicate with anyone, anywhere in the world, any time.

The first WANs were on-line services such as Prodigy, CompuServe, and America Online. They allowed thousands of users to connect simultaneously by telephone to a central system that provides electronic information.

The Internet is a worldwide system of networks that allows users on one network to reach users on other networks. Internet is the largest network in the world. It contains more than 14,000 other networks that offer a huge variety of services, and it reaches more than 15 million people.

What does all this mean to you? It means that you will increasingly be using computers and related devices when you communicate. This will be true regardless of the occupational path you follow.

Communication 2000, "Module 1: Workplace Communication," (1996). Cincinnati: OH: South-Western Educational Publishing.

The Internet Keeps Growing

The Internet is an on-line computer network that spans the globe. Millions of computers are already hooked up to it, and a thousand more go on-line every day. It's changing the way people communicate with one another more dramatically than anything since the invention of the telephone.

The Internet began in 1969 when the Department of Defense wanted a communication network that could survive an atomic-missile attack. A tiny network of 50 computers was set up around the world to link military officials. Later the Internet was opened to the public, and, with the development of inexpensive personal computers, use has skyrocketed. As of 1995, more than 20 million people were using the network daily, according to the International Internet Association.

The Internet can be used for many different activities. To gain access, you can sign up with an on-line company such as CompuServe, America Online, or Prodigy. These companies charge a monthly fee to connect individuals and businesses to the network. Once on-line, you can communicate directly with other people by typing messages on your keyboard and reading their words on your screen. Got something you need to tell the President? His electronic-mail address is *president@whitehouse.gov*.

A total of 20,000 sub-networks are wired into the Internet. Want to sell your car? Commerce Net is an electronic marketplace that can put buyers and sellers in immediate contact with one another. You can tap into numerous databases, even the Library of Congress. There are many electronic bulletin boards—whatever your interest, from politics to chess to dancing to job-hunting, you can probably find a bulletin board that specializes in it. There are even electronic magazines and books that can be read on the Internet. But the most popular use of the Internet is e-mail, with more than two-thirds of the subscribers using the network for direct communication.

Communication 2000, "Module 1: Workplace Communication," (1996). Cincinnati: OH: South-Western Educational Publishing.

Appendix B

Common Prefixes, Suffixes, and Roots

Common Prefixes

PREFIX	EXAMPLE	MEANING
a-, an-	amoral	not, without, lacking
ab, a-, abs-	abhor	away from
ad-, ac-, af-, ag-, al-, an-, ap-, ar-, as-, at-	adhere	toward
ambi-	ambivalence	both
amphi-	amphitheater	on both sides, around
ante-	antebellum	before
anti-	antibiotic	against
auto-	automatic	self
bi-	bisect	two
centi-	century	hundred
circum-	circumstance	around
con-, com-, co-, col-, cor-	correlate	with, in association, together
contra-	contradiction	against
de-	descend	away from, out of, separation
dec-, deca-	decade	ten
di-	dicotyledon	two, twice, double
dia-	diameter	through, between, across
dis-	dissatisfied	not
ex-, e-, ef-	evict	out of, from
for-	forehand	away, off, wrong
fore-	forefront	before, front, superior
hemi-	hemisphere	half
hepta-	heptagon	seven
hexa-	hexagon	six
hyper-	hypersensitive	over, above
in-, il-, ir-, im-	invisible, invade	not, also means in and is used as an intensifier
inter-	interact	between, among
intra-, intro-	introvert	within
kilo-	kilocycle	thousand
milli-	millennium	thousand
mis-	misspell	wrong, not
mono-	monopoly	one
multi-	multitude	many
non-	nonsense	not
nona-	nonagon	nine
ob-, oc-, of-	obstruct	toward, to, on, over, against
oct-	octagon	eight
omni-	omnipotent	all
pan-	pantheist	all
per-	perceive	through, thoroughly, very

pro-	promote	in favor of, advancing
quadr-	quadrupled	four
quin-	quintuplet	five
re-	reorganize	backward, again
retro-	retrograde	backward
se-	select	apart
semi-	semiannual	half
sept-	September	seven
sex-	sextant	six
sub-, suc-, suf-, sur-, sug-, sus-	supplant	under, below, slightly
super-	supercede	above, beyond
syn-, sym-	synchronize	with, together
tele-	telegraph	distance
tetra-	tetrameter	four
trans-, tra-	traverse	across, beyond, through
tri-	triple	three
ultra-	ultramodern	beyond, farther
un-	unnatural	not
uni-	unilateral	one

Common Suffixes

SUFFIX	EXAMPLE	MEANING
-able, -ible	durable, visible	able
-acy	piracy, privacy	quality, state, office
-age	breakage, orphanage	pertaining to; also, a noun-forming suffix
-al	rental, abdominal	adjective- or noun- forming suffix
-ance, -ence	insurance, competence	adjective- or noun- forming suffix
-ant	reliant, servant	adjective- or noun- forming suffix
-arium, -orium	aquarium, auditorium	place, instrument
-ary	dictionary, elementary	pertaining to, connected with
-ate	activate, animate	verb-forming suffix used with English nouns
-ation, -ition	creation, condition	combination of -ate and -ion used for forming nouns
-cle, -icle	corpuscle, denticle	small, diminutive
-esque	picturesque	style, manner, distinctive character
-ferous	coniferous	bearing
-ful	colorful	full of

-fy, -ify	fortify, magnify	to make, to cause to be
-hood	childhood, statehood	state, condition, nature
-ic	democratic, phonic	suffix forming adjectives from nouns
-ism	conservatism, Marxism	used to form nouns denoting action, practice, principles, doctrines
-itis	appendicitis	inflammation, abnormal state or condition
-ity	acidity, familiarity	used to form nouns expressing state or condition
-ive	creative, suggestive	suffix of adjectives expressing tendancy, disposition, function
-ize	memorize, modernize	verb suffix
-ment	statement	denotes an action, resulting state, product
-mony	testimony, parsimony	result or condition, denotes action or condition
-oid	avoid, ellipsoid	resembling, like
-or	conqueror, generator	one who does something
-ose, -ous	verbose, porous	full of
-osis	hypnosis	denotes action, state, process, or condition
-tude	solitude, altitude	indicates nouns formed from adjectives

Common Roots

ROOT	EXAMPLE	MEANING
ag, act	activate, enact, agile, energy	to do
anthrop	anthropology, anthropomorphic, misanthrope	man
aqua	aquifer, aquatic, aquueous	water
aud	audible, audition, auditorium, audience	hear
auto	automatic, automation, automaton	self
bene	benefit, benevolent, benign	good
cap, capt, chap	decapitate, capture, captain, chapter	head
ceed, cede, cess	proceed, precedent, cease	go, yield
chrom	chromatic, chromosome	color
chron	synchronize, chronology, chronic	time
cogn	cognition, recognize, cognitive	know
corp	corporate, corpulent, corporation	body
cred	credit, incredible, credulous	belief
dent, dont	orthodontist, dental, dentifrice	tooth
derm	dermatology, epidermis, dermatitis	skin
dic, dict	dictionary, dictate, predict, indict	say
don, donat	donate, donor, condone, pardon	to give
dox	doxology, paradox	belief
duc	duct, reduct, produce, conduct	lead in
fac, fic, fy	manufacture, factory verify	make, do
fer	transfer, ferry, confer, defer, suffer	bear
fid	confident, infidel, confide	faith

fluc, flux	fluctuate, fluxion	flow
graph	graphite, telegraph, phonograph	write
gress	transgress, congress, egress	step
ject	deject, rejection, conjecture, trajectory	throw
loc	local, locate, location, dislocate	place
loq, loc	eloquent, elocution, interlocutor	speak
mal	malevolent, malapropism, malefactor	bad
manu	manufacture, manuscript, manacle, manual	hand
miso, misa	misanthrope, misogamy	bad
mit, mis	emit, permit, dismissal, omit, missile	send
morph	morphology, endomorph, metamorphosis	shape
mort	mortician, mortuary, mortify	dead
mov, mot, mob	motivate, motion, motile, remove	move
neb	nebulous, nebula	cloudy
omni	omnipresent, omniscient, omnipotent	all
path	sympathy, empathic, pathetic	suffering, disease, feeling
ped	pedestrian, pedometer, pedicure	foot
phil	philosophy, philanthropy, philharmonic	love
pod	podiatrist, pseudopod	foot
scrib, script	transcript, prescribe, description	write

Appendix C

Reading Charts, Graphs and Maps

This section will allow you to practice the skill of interpreting charts, graphs, and maps. It also provides brief instructions on how to get the most out of these visual tools that are found in most textbooks and workplace documents. First, read the following information on how to interpret visual data. Then, practice with the visual graphics provided in this appendix, or use those that are in other textbooks from the courses you are now taking.

When To Use Graphics

Visual graphics such as charts, graphs, and maps can help you to better understand material you are reading. Like "mind maps" (Chapter 3) they can help you to organize and interpret a great deal of information at a glance. The key to using them effectively is to use them before, during, and after reading the text that goes with them.

Before reading, graphics can prepare you for what you are about to read by conveying certain ideas and relationships that will be expressed in the reading. By studying graphics ahead of time, you are able to understand some of the main points of the reading even before you start. Thus, you are preparing your mind to receive the information in the text. *During reading,* graphics should be used as a reference to clarify any thoughts you might have about the relationships they describe. Good readers frequently glance back and forth between the text that they are reading and pictures or other graphics to help in understanding.

Finally, *after reading,* graphics can be used as study aids since they usually contain many or most of the main ideas expressed in the text. Instead of having to reread the text, you can use the graphics to refresh your memory about important relationships and information expressed. The result is that you will spend less time studying and re-reading the material.

How To Interpret Graphics

The process of interpreting graphics is very similar to the process of reading. You first prepare by thinking about what you already know about the information presented. Then, you ask questions or make predictions. Finally, you interpret the data presented, thinking about how it might relate to the knowledge you had beforehand. To make this process easier, follow these steps:

1. *Identify the main idea* of the graphic. Look at the title (and subtitle if it has one). Think about what you already know about the topic.

2. *Read the legend or key.* These are usually located in the margins of the graphic, either at the top, the bottom, or on one side. Study any symbols, abbreviations, or colors that might have meaning.

3. *Ask questions* about what you might find out from this chart, map, or graph. (If you already know a good deal about the topic, predict what you will find in it.) What kinds of information are provided? Think about what you want to learn from it, or ask, "What do I think the author might include in this?"

4. ***Interpret the information.*** Use the symbols, numbers, colors, etc. to look for relationships, draw conclusions, and make inferences.

Even though this looks like a lot of work, the process described here really takes only a few moments, and it becomes easier the more you practice. Remember to use the process before, during, and after the reading that goes with it. You will see that it helps you to understand the text better, and you will also see that how you interpret the data is affected by what you are reading. You may see relationships during and after reading that you missed in your first viewing.

What to Look For in Different Types of Maps, Graphs, and Tables

Bar Graphs (Figure 1) illustrate differences in quantities by the lengths of the bars in the graph. It is easy to identify the differences between the items.

Figure 1

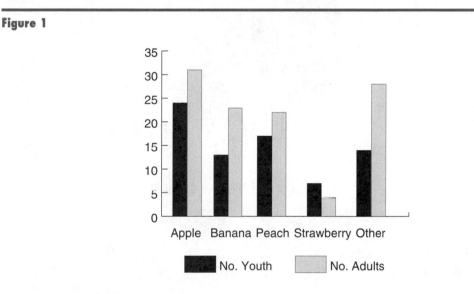

FLAVOR PREFERENCES

FLAVOR	NO. YOUTH	NO. ADULTS
Apple	24	31
Banana	13	23
Peach	17	22
Strawberry	7	4
Other	14	28

Clark, Allen, and Klooster. *Computers and Information Processing: Concepts and Applications*, (1990). Cincinnati, Ohio: South-Western, p. 278.

1. What is the main idea of this bar graph?

2. What two groups of people are compared?

3. What conclusions can you make about people's favorite fruit flavors?

Pie Charts divide a circle graph into segments that resemble different sized slices of pie (Figure 2). They are most useful to show how the parts of a whole are distributed and how the parts relate to each other.

Figure 2

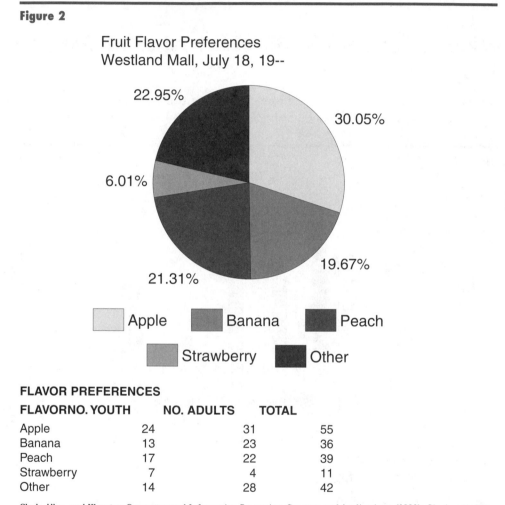

Fruit Flavor Preferences
Westland Mall, July 18, 19--

FLAVOR PREFERENCES

FLAVOR	NO. YOUTH	NO. ADULTS	TOTAL
Apple	24	31	55
Banana	13	23	36
Peach	17	22	39
Strawberry	7	4	11
Other	14	28	42

Clark, Allen, and Klooster. *Computers and Information Processing: Concepts and Applications*. (1990). Cincinnati, Ohio: South-Western, p. 279.

1. What is the main idea of this graph?

2. How does the key differ from that of the bar graph in Figure 1?

3. How does the information in the pie chart differ from that of the bar graph in Figure 1?

Line Graphs (Figures 3 and 4) show how data varies over time. Typically, the side measures the quantity of what is being measured, while the bottom measures time in hours, weeks, months, years, etc. By looking at any point on a line on the chart, and reading straight over to both side and bottom, you can tell what the quantity was at a specific time. When more than one line is presented, you can see the relationship of another variable. In Figure 3, the dotted line represents dollar sales of hotdogs in different months, and the solid line represents dollar sales of yogurt over the same time period.

Figure 3

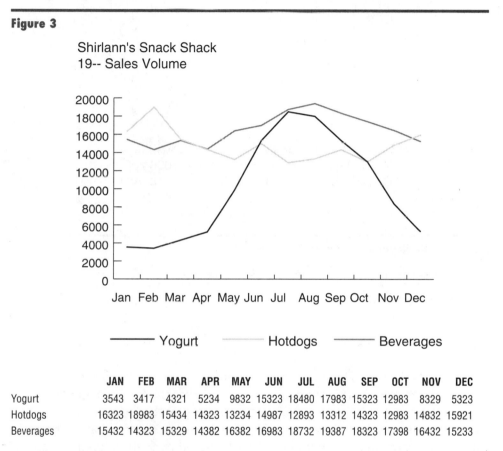

Shirlann's Snack Shack
19-- Sales Volume

	JAN	FEB	MAR	APR	MAY	JUN	JUL	AUG	SEP	OCT	NOV	DEC
Yogurt	3543	3417	4321	5234	9832	15323	18480	17983	15323	12983	8329	5323
Hotdogs	16323	18983	15434	14323	13234	14987	12893	13312	14323	12983	14832	15921
Beverages	15432	14323	15329	14382	16382	16983	18732	19387	18323	17398	16432	15233

Clark, Allen, and Klooster. *Computers and Information Processing: Concepts and Applications*, (1990). Cincinnati, Ohio: South-Western, p. 280.

1. What is the main idea of the line chart shown here?

2. Which of the items is more seasonal than the other two?

3. How might the vendor use the data shown?

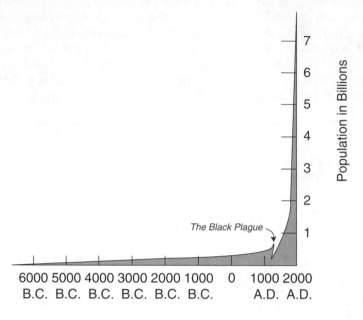

Camp and Daugherty. *Managing Our Natural Resources*, (1991). Delmar, p. 26.

Figure 4   World population over 8,000 years

1. What is the main idea of the chart shown here?

2. Has the growth in the population over the years been steady on our planet?

3. What conclusions can you draw from this chart?

Area Charts (Figure 5) combine the characteristics of other types of charts and graphs to present information. You can see that the first chart in Figure 5 looks like a bar graph because it shows quantities by the length of the bar. However, it is also a bit like a pie chart since each bar shows what portion of the total is made up of the component parts, noted by their colors. The bottom chart, in similar fashion, combines the characteristics of a line graph and a pie chart.

Figure 5

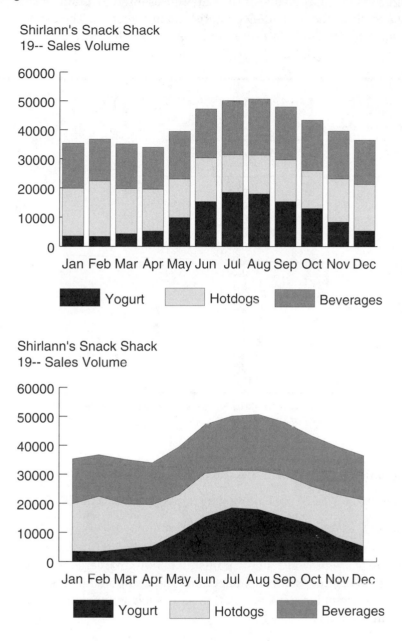

Shirlann's Snack Shack
19-- Sales Volume

Shirlann's Snack Shack
19-- Sales Volume

Clark, Allen, and Klooster. *Computers and Information Processing: Concepts and Applications.* (1990) Cincinnati, Ohio: South-Western, p. 281.

1. How are area charts similar to both pie charts and either bar graphs or line graphs?

2. Which of the charts in this figure would be easier to read? Why?

3. What conclusions can be drawn from these charts?

Tables (Figure 6) are typed or printed displays of words or numbers arranged in columns and rows. A quick glance at the data represented in a table can make for easy and clear understanding of statistical information. The same techniques should be applied in interpreting them before, during, and after the reading.

Figure 6

TABLE 3-1
World Population over 8000 Years[1]

Year	World population (in billions)
6000 B.C.	0.01
1 A.D.	0.25
1500 A.D.	0.50
1750 A.D.	0.79
1800 A.D.	0.98
1900 A.D.	1.65
1950 A.D.	2.49
1960 A.D.	3.0
1965 A.D.	3.3
1970 A.D.	3.7
1975 A.D.	4.0
1978 A.D.	4.2
1979 A.D.	4.3
2000 A.D. (projected)	6.5
2050 A.D. (projected)	11.0

[1]Sources: United Nations, *The World Population Situation in 1970;* United States Department of the Interior, *Yearbook No. 2—The Population Challenge.*

Camp and Daugherty. *Managing Our Natural Resources,* (1991). Delmar, p. 25.

1. What information is provided in this table that is not given in Figure 4?

2. Which of the two forms of presenting data is easier to read quickly?

3. Which provides data that you can manipulate mathematically?

Schematic drawings are drawings of diagrams that show an overall view of a mechanism, system, or process with connections and components labeled. These graphics are useful for showing relationships such as the sources of pollution in Figures 7 and 8.

Figure 7

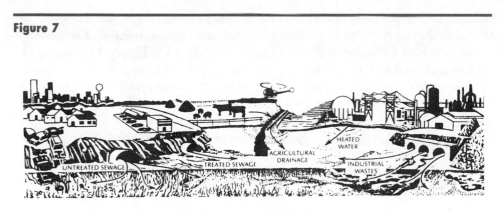

Camp and Daugherty. *Managing Our Natural Resources*, (1991). Delmar, p. 121.

1. How would a quick study of this diagram help prepare you to read a chapter on waste management?

2. What is not shown here about pollutants that might be provided in a table or bar graph?

3. What conclusions can be drawn from this drawing?

Figure 8

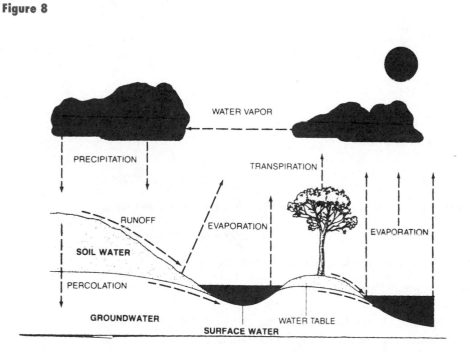

Camp and Daugherty. *Managing Our Natural Resources,* (1991). Delmar, p. 106.

Explain why this drawing is a good example of the expression, "A picture says a thousand words."

Maps (Figure 9) can convey enormous amounts of information about geographic relationships. The important thing for you to do is to study the information provided in the headings and margins. The map in Figure 9 shows location and condition of nuclear reactors in the United States. It also displays the electricity production capacity for all plants. Without reading the key or legend, maps are of little value. Different maps display different sorts of information. For another example, open a history or geography book and find a map. What kinds of information are provided in it? How does that information relate to the chapter in which you found the map?

Figure 9

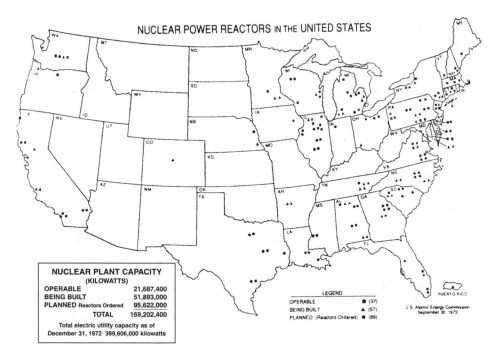

Camp and Donahue. *Environmental Science For Agriculture and the Life Sciences.* (1994). Delmar, p. 171.

1. What information is given along the margins of this map?

2. Are there more nuclear plants in operation or planned?

3. What conclusions might you draw from this information?

Remember that charts, maps, and graphs can be of great value in helping you to understand your textbooks and more technical reading like articles, instructions, and reports. Follow the simple steps in interpreting them at the different stages of reading to add to your success in reading.

Index